Inspired Pragmatism

An Illustrated History of Linfield College

Inspired Pragmatism
An Illustrated History of Linfield College

Marvin Henberg

Edited and Afterword by
Barbara Kitt Seidman

Carpe Diem Books®

10 9 8 7 6 5 4 3 2 1

Published by:
Carpe Diem Books
8136 N.W. Skyline Boulevard
Portland, Oregon 97229
www.carpediembooks.com

Design: Reynolds Wulf Inc.
Robert Reynolds, Letha Wulf
Copyediting: Judy McNally
Index: Cher Paul
Manufacturing: Dick Owsiany
Project coordinator: Ross Eberman

Manufactured in China

Cover: *2007, Pioneer Hall cupola at dusk*
Page 2: *2006, Aerial view of campus from the northwest, looking southeast*
Pages 4 and 5: *2007, Oak grove on a spring morning*
Page 8: *1909-10, The McMinnville College logo on display in this montage of the men's basketball team. The coach (wearing tie) is Edgar B. Van Osdel, professor of chemistry and physics, and director of the observatory. The players, named in archival rosters but not individually identified, are J. Foster, William Foster, E.F. McKee, H.L. McCabe, V.D. Miller, Ray Cammack, and R.S. McKee.*
Page 9: *2007, Branches of the Old Oak shade Pioneer Hall steps.*
Page 10: *2007, Melrose Hall*
Page 11: *2007, Students take advantage of inviting study space inside the new Jereld R. Nicholson Library.*
Page 12: (Left) *2007, Karen Shaw, front, and Jennifer Johnson pursue collaborative research in the lab of Assistant Professor of Biology Anne Kruchten.* (Top right) *2007, Assistant Professor of Mathematics Charles Dunn, left, works out a problem with Gabe Haberly.* (Bottom right) *2007, Left to right: Renata Tirta, Patrick Maxwell, and Miyuki Hayashi search among the more than 28.6 million volumes available online in Nicholson Library.*
Page 13: (Top) *Smiles over "The Linfield Experience" alive and well in the twenty-first century.* (Bottom left) *2007, A quiet moment in "The Nic"– Nicholson Library.* (Bottom right) *2007, Tyler McCann pursues collaborative research in the lab of Associate Professor of Chemistry Elizabeth Atkinson.*
Page 14: *2003, Wildcats quarterback Tyler Matthews sprints out to pass against Pacific Lutheran.*
Page 15: *2007, Adjunct Professor of Music Stephen Kravitz rehearses an ensemble in the new Vivian A. Bull Music Center.*
Page 16: *1908-09, McMinnville College group picture*
Back Cover: *1903-04, McMinnville College students and faculty on the steps of Pioneer Hall*

Photography credits:
Tom Ballard, pages 124, 138
Kelly Bird, pages 14, 121, 122, 127
Reid Blackburn, page 89
Juan Calvillo, pages 2, 133
Doug Cruickshank, page 88
Ryan Gardner, page 120 (right)
Jerome Hart, pages 13 (top), 123
Daniel Hurst, page 125
Oliver Ogden, page 129
Sally Painter, pages 110, 132
Rick Rappaport, pages 112, 115
Robert Reynolds, pages Cover, 2, 4-5, 10, 12, 13 (bottom), 15, 108, 109, 128, 130, 131, 136-137, 139, 140

All others from Linfield College archives, no photographer identified.

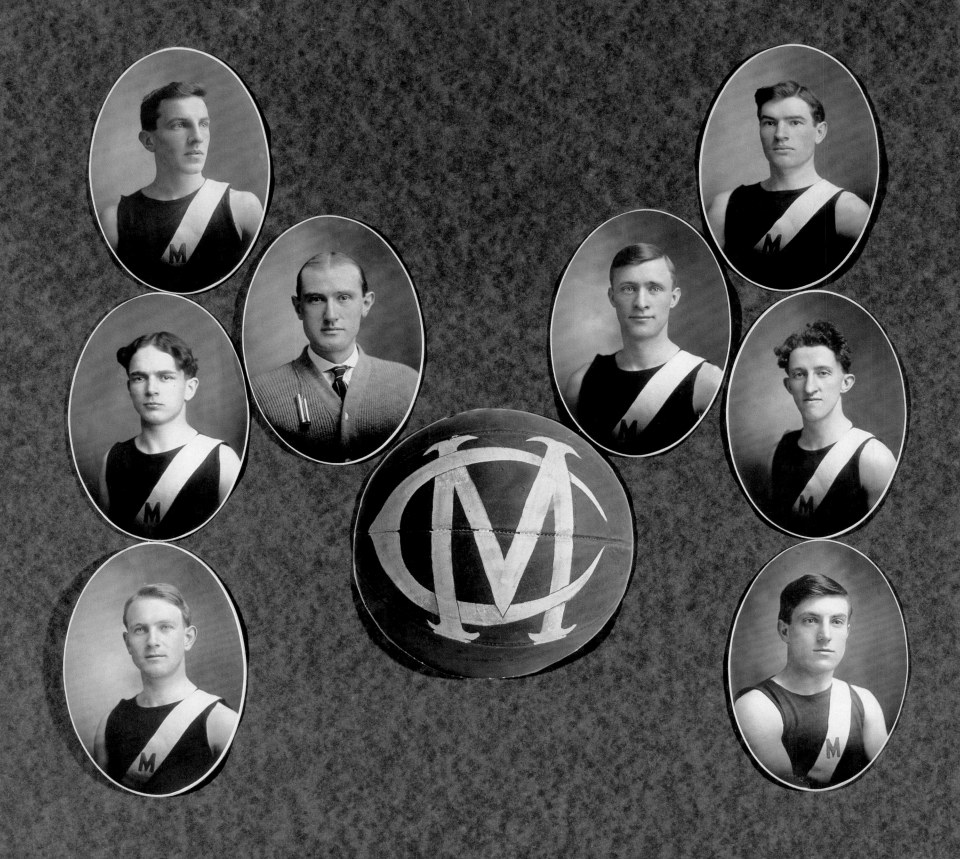

Contents

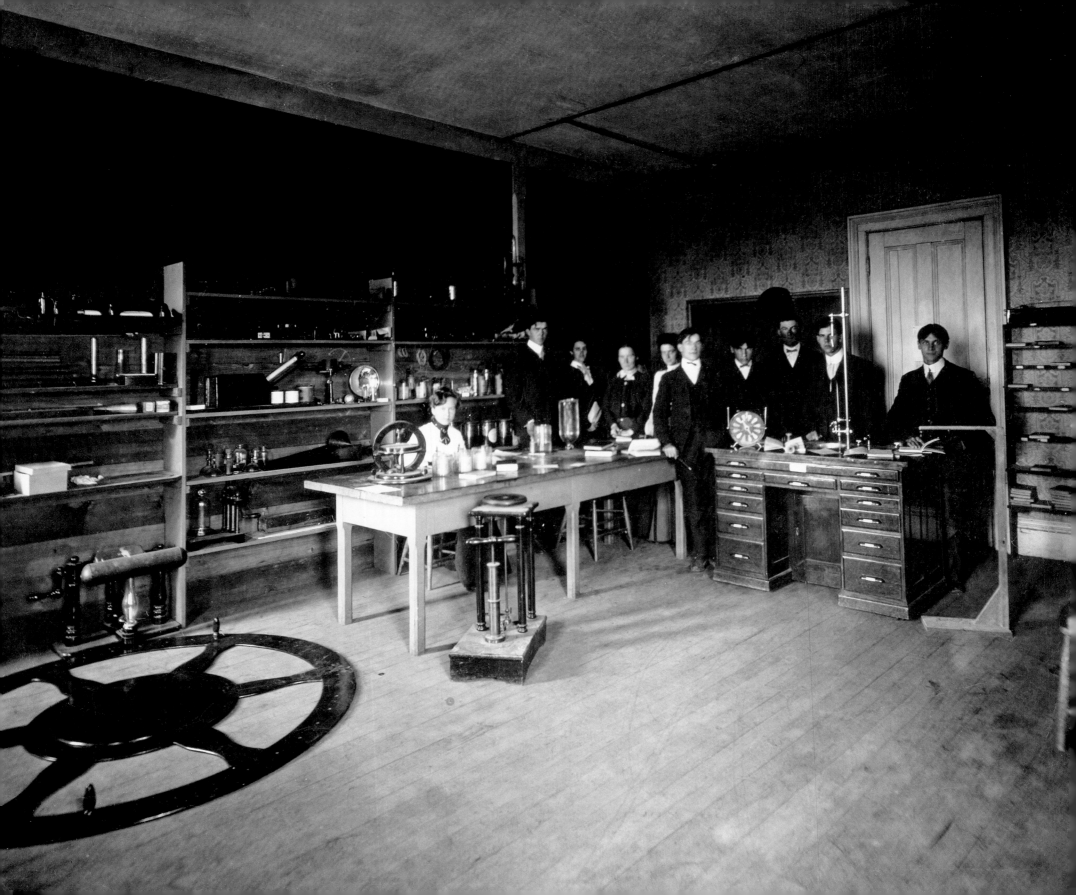

Preface
One Hundred Fifty Years and Counting

History regularly reminds us that what we think we know about the familiar world we inhabit falls considerably short of the full story. Linfield College circa 2007 offers just such complications to the student of its past—its very name has changed over time as a result of shifting circumstances. And yet the core educational vision that

Rev. George C. Chandler, president of Oregon City College
Oregon Historical Society CN 003469

Opposite: *1890s, Early science class in Pioneer Hall*

led to its creation in the mid-nineteenth century not only has remained intact but has continued to transform the lives of those who enter its orbit. This volume documents and celebrates that cohesiveness of purpose.

Linfield's origins extend back to the early days of American-claimed Oregon itself. On January 30, 1858, the Oregon Territory granted a charter to The Baptist College at McMinnville. In 1898, the Board of Trustees filed new articles of incorporation formally changing the name to McMinnville College. "Old Mac," its nickname for over fifty years, became Linfield College in 1922, in honor of George Fisher Linfield, whose widow bestowed on the school a substantial gift of property in exchange for the renaming. Friends of the college celebrate its sesquicentennial on January 30, 2008.

Human institutions rarely endure, let alone thrive, for so long. For instance, only 6 percent of corporations on the 2006 Fortune 500 list existed in 1856. Even fewer could claim to have resided in the same city throughout a hundred-and-fifty-year history. Place has clearly played a central role in the story of Linfield College. Both city and college grew up on the frontier and embodied the sturdy spirit of their founding pioneers. In 1856 Joel B. Palmer, superintendent of Indian affairs for the Oregon Territory, formally negotiated with the Yam Hill band of Calapooya Indians to relinquish the land now occupied by McMinnville. The first white settlers discovered an agricultural Eden in the Willamette Valley, given its stark contrast to so much of the arid West. McMinn-

ville itself came into being in 1856, only two years before the college's charter was issued in 1858.

Identifying Linfield's actual founding date requires further historical clarification, however. Because its name had included explicit reference to McMinnville for its first sixty-plus years, Linfield chose to celebrate its own centennial year in 1956 to coincide with the city's centennial year. To confuse the matter of origins even further, the college trustees who planned the 1956 centennial laid equal claim to 1849, since in that year Baptists had established its predecessor school in Oregon City and hired George Chandler to lead it. A few years later, upon its relocation to the Yamhill Valley, Chandler became the first president of The Baptist College at McMinnville.

Each of the above founding dates emphasizes a different portion of Linfield's story. Those who pick 1849 may choose to emphasize its place within the saga of Baptist proselytizing in the West. Those who select 1856 may lean toward the search of McMinnville cofounders William Newby and Sebastian Adams for a college to serve their town. Those who identify 1858 as its originating moment may prefer to focus on the civic rather than denominational aims of its early adherents.

While the narrative whole that constitutes Linfield's history remains richly informed by the aspirations and recollections of its myriad participants, all alumni and friends of the college hold dear a distinctive "Linfield Experience" composed of singular memories unrecorded in the college archives. No author trying to convey the basic shape of the college's history can know even a fraction of such stories, let alone record them here. While hoping to avoid anything that diminishes cherished memories, I have confined myself to studying thousands of documents that have helped me discover overarching truths that illuminate the last hundred and fifty years. For the most part I have avoided anecdotes and oral histories. I have done so because I could not begin to manage a quest for such information. Instead I have relied on printed materials that offer pieces of the official story—trustee minutes, presidential and faculty correspondence, written reminiscences, newspapers, college catalogs, college annuals, books, and journals. Because these sources remain available to all, others may inspect them and draw their own conclusions, as with any legitimate historical undertaking.

In that regard, I have an important caveat to make. To reserve as much space as possible for the college's narrative and pictorial story, I have omitted bibliographic details and footnotes from this text. Interested readers will find printed copies of all such citations in the archives of Nicholson Library. Electronic copies are available on the Linfield website at www.linfield.edu/pragmatism.

America in 1858

Selecting the charter date of 1858 as the point of origin for Linfield College foregrounds the institution's role in the evolving civic character of the Oregon frontier. The territorial and state legislators of the region chartered many colleges of varying types to assure that citizens would have opportunities for education according to their preferences. Thus they authorized schools with denominational as well as nondenominational, private as well as public, characters. This educational philosophy, aimed at fostering free choice among free persons, has served the college productively in the past and most assuredly will do so into the future.

The pragmatism influencing Oregon's civic leaders at the time of Linfield's founding sprang from their awareness that the main focus of the nation in 1858 lay thousands of miles to the east, its outermost edge defined by the shores of the Mississippi River. With the Civil War already looming, the business of crafting and admitting new partners to the Union continued apace, with such "western" states as Minnesota granted statehood in the same year of 1858 that marked Linfield's charter. Oregon itself did not attain statehood until the next year, on February 14, 1859.

Albeit far away, the political turmoil swirling around the expanding Union did indeed resonate out to the Pacific coast, not least because every new state contributed to the precarious balancing act between slave and free states that served as one deterrent to full-fledged Southern secession. As a way of situating Linfield's founding within that national picture, one might note that in the same year of its charter, the famous Lincoln-Douglas debates occurred in September and October 1858. Newspapers across the country reprinted the full text of each debate, and readers everywhere flocked to purchase and read them. While the debates unfolded as part of Illinois' Senate race, they thrust Lincoln into national prominence and paved the way for his presidential election in 1860—the event that finally triggered rebellion. The Civil War was only the first of several wars that would threaten the college's enrollment and financial stability across its history. Moreover, the war gave prominence to the question of racial justice, of relevance not only to the frontier Baptists involved in Linfield's founding but also to subsequent college leaders concerned with expanding educational access for all.

The slavery issue posed just one example of the debates arising among Oregon Baptists in the vexed pursuit of doctrinal orthodoxy. Linfield, as one of their fledgling institutions, frequently experienced such struggles since its educational mandate made the stakes that much higher for the faculty and the student body. An important theme in this narrative centers on the scope of free expression deemed appropriate on a religiously affiliated college campus. The intensity of such debates might best be exemplified by the continuing turmoil generated around another signal event of 1858. On July 1, Charles Darwin and Alfred Russell Wallace jointly presented their papers on evolution at a London meeting of the Linnaean Society. Their ideas clearly threatened Bishop Ussher's famous estimate that the world had been created in 4004 B.C.–a belief widely accepted at the time in the United States as well as in Europe. Not surprisingly, concern over the teaching of evolutionary theory would prompt harsh rhetoric and even action by many Baptist supporters of Linfield over the coming years. What differentiated Linfield's Baptists from other opponents of the "New Thinking" remained a commitment to freedom of conscience that justified academic freedom and faculty autonomy, albeit in decidedly constricted ways by contemporary standards.

Finally, one must remember that for all these links to complex national and international debates of the time, Linfield came into being as part of the Northwest frontier, and therefore its daily world remained acutely circumscribed and primarily local. News from afar proved hard to get and took time to obtain. Linfield's few students from outside the area traveled to McMinnville by horse and horse-drawn carriage. They communicated home via handwritten letter conveyed by the postal service. Certainly technology had begun to change the possibilities for broader and more immediate communication, but progress unfolded slowly and reached the hinterlands more slowly still. Though President James Buchanan did indeed exchange telegraphed greetings with Queen Victoria in 1858 via a newly laid transatlantic cable, the success and scope of the event ended when, a few months later, the original cable went silent and required complete rebuilding. Thus, as technology expanded, its reliability posed problems. Throughout its history, the small rural college that became Linfield has found its horizons steadily expanded by technological innovations in transportation and communication that have made it a true global citizen.

In all of these ways Linfield might be regarded as a quintessential American creation born of a particular time and place through the converging visions of groups with different agendas but common values. It also stands as an example of one of America's signature institutional inventions–the private liberal arts college. These distinctive American roots provide the book's title, for Linfield College offers a striking case study in what I am calling Inspired Pragmatism.

Inspired Pragmatism

The faith inspiring the founders of The Baptist College at McMinnville emphasized freedom of conscience for each believer. Like many other devout American Christians before them, they regarded their westering as "an errand into the wilderness." Historian Perry Miller derived this phrase from a 1670 Massachusetts sermon to characterize a central theme of the American experience: a quest to save souls for Christ. Linfield's Baptist supporters shared this aim, but their doctrine provided them wider latitude than many other Christians. Freedom of conscience required that an individual's progress toward salvation be genuinely self-willed: otherwise it lacked value. Baptist precept made clear that no person may require from another a protestation of faith.

The "Northern Baptists" who founded Linfield identified in letter and spirit with Roger Williams, Baptist founder of Rhode Island whose cause of religious liberty later inspired the First Amendment of the U.S. Constitution. Linfield proudly stands among such institutions as Brown University, the University of Chicago, Kalamazoo College, and the University of Redlands, all products of Northern Baptist educational zeal. Because Linfield's leadership remained more conservative than many sister institutions until the social upheavals of the 1960s, its faculty and students have periodically been judged as errant in the ways of the Baptist faith. Still, Linfield presidents have generally defended freedom of conscience and won the day with restive boards and community leaders. Even when a president in 1946 endorsed dubious findings from a Special Committee on Religious Education and Investigation, his intrusion upon academic freedom exerted little lasting impact.

If Linfield's founders acted from a zeal to realize God's

kingdom on earth, they sought just as diligently to make the Northwest a better place in concrete, worldly ways. Their labors coincided with the emergence of pragmatism as America's defining philosophical movement. A term first used in 1878 by Charles Sanders Peirce, pragmatism focuses on the practical consequences of human thought. For Peirce, beliefs functioned as rules for action (*pragma* in Greek). His test for the meaning of any thought lay in asking what consequences it would produce in conduct. Pragmatism emphasizes the useful, an American trait par excellence and a necessity among those creating a new society in the West, as historian Frederick Jackson Turner observed in his seminal 1893 essay, "The Significance of the Frontier in American History."

Exemplifying the habits of mind that underscored this American philosophical outlook, Linfield has long defined its goals in terms of the practical. Though the founders had to wait for their "college" (since the first bachelor's degree was not awarded until 1884), that did not keep them from establishing primary and secondary departments to teach skills badly needed on the frontier: reading, writing, elocution, and arithmetic. Just as pragmatically, the college, from its inception, not only admitted both men and women students but hired male and female faculty members. This commitment, too, reflects a frontier heritage. It simply did not occur to Linfield's founders to establish the kind of single-sex college predominant in the East and the South. An egalitarian spirit still evident at Linfield took root in the demand for as many trained hands as possible to "civilize" the wilderness. In a more mundane sense, the college's pragmatism led to an early reliance on student labor that continues to this day. The first recorded printer employed by the college was a student who earned his tuition by practicing his useful art. Union organizers in the 1950s objected to the college's habitual use of student labor to construct its buildings. Today's essential computers and software would crash once and for all without student help in maintaining them. Whenever financial resources have been scarce, Linfield's leaders have turned for help to its principal constituency.

Linfield's strain of frugality runs deep, as does its outreach to students of modest means and its dedication to preparing students for productive lives. Witness a concluding epigram from a 1960s document on the future: "Faith and unstinted effort, as in the past, will continue to set the course of Linfield College toward greater usefulness." A gospel of practicality has informed the institutional mission as thoroughly as the redemptive Gospel of the college's Baptist founders.

Such pragmatic orientation finds reinforcement in Linfield's adoption of the principles of the American liberal arts college, one of the defining innovations of U.S. history. In contrast to nineteenth-century Britain, where liberal education consciously signaled class privilege through its concentration on classical languages, the American variant has deep egalitarian roots. American colleges initially embraced the British emphasis on the classics, but with two main differences. First, as at McMinnville College, liberal learning permitted each student a wide subject range, whereas British and continental European students necessarily specialized in a single subject from the outset. Second, America's equivocal attitude toward European values and civilization could not tolerate exclusivist assumptions. Americans began to think of liberal education as "liberating," unleashing powers inherent in every individual. In this regard, liberal education–however arcane the subject matter–fostered a democratic citizenry. Rather than adopt Britain's class-bound heritage, American educational leaders viewed learning through the lens of social mobility. Why shouldn't the sons and daughters of poor families aspire to improve their prospects in life alongside those who already enjoyed wealth?

Thanks to this emphasis on broadened access, liberal arts colleges dot the landscape of America in much the same way that commercial centers spread out at a day's horse ride from each other–or, in sparser country, at intervals permitting a train's steam engine to refuel. Oregon proved no exception. Every emerging community–Oregon City to McMinnville,

Corvallis to Albany, Portland to Salem—wanted its own college. Every Christian denomination also sought to ensure its future by establishing a local school, as much for an ongoing supply of trained clergy as for service to the lay community. Linfield sprang from an intersection of these secular and denominational impulses.

Though much of Linfield's history has involved the management of tensions between liberal education and sectarian loyalty, such struggles have subsided today. By the twenty-first century, the college's original denominational affiliation has become less and less central to its mission, its classroom activity, and its students. Very few of today's students self-identify as Baptist or American Baptist: 3 or 4 percent in McMinnville and less than 1 percent in Portland. The denominational affiliation most cited by contemporary Linfield students (roughly 10 percent) is Roman Catholic.

From a doctrinal standpoint, then, the secularized college that exists today might disappoint the men and women, including Mrs. Frances Ross Linfield, who nurtured it along the way and often rescued it from closure. But this history proudly documents the college's originating impulse in Baptist freedom of conscience. The tireless spirit of free inquiry that the Baptists bequeathed to Linfield has over time fostered a broad, ecumenical perspective well suited to the challenges of modern life.

Inspired pragmatism, then, emphasizes practical wisdom at the same time that it honors the force and persistence of idealism. Linfield's story provides a superb example of this philosophy in action. Its future remains secure so long as it finds inspiration in what is useful and usefully seeks inspiration.

A Note on Organization

Following this introduction, the book unfolds in four chapters and an afterword written by Barbara Kitt Seidman. The first chapter—"The Story Retold"—narrates the college's history from its beginnings until 1932. College historian Dr. Jonas A. Jonasson covers this period in *Bricks Without Straw*,

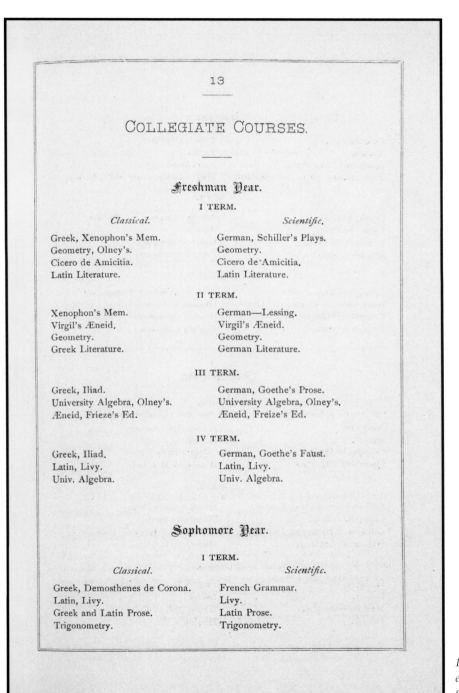

1872-73, Page from first extant McMinnville College catalog

published in 1938. I retell his story in many fewer words, with a bit of amplification where needed. My debt to Jonasson (see "Servant Historians," p. 86) is enormous and will become obvious to anyone who reads his fine book.

Chapter 2–"The Untold Story"–covers the time from 1932, when Dr. Elam Anderson became president, until 1974, when his great-nephew Dr. Gordon Bjork resigned the presidency. This part of the story still exists within memory of living alumni but stands far enough removed in time to constitute history rather than contemporary reporting.

"The Parallel Story," subject of chapter 3, returns to Oregon's pioneer past to tell the story of Good Samaritan Hospital and its school of nursing, which in 1982 became part of the Linfield saga. Finally, chapter 4, "The Unfolding Story," covers the presidencies of Dr. Charles U. Walker and Dr. Vivian A. Bull. Events in this period remain current enough that the story functions as much as journalism as history. Since the author becomes a part of the Linfield story during this period, I cannot claim the same degree of independence and objectivity as I have attempted with the earlier chapters. At best, then, I offer a "first draft of history" in chapter 4, anticipating that some future scholar will put these events in broader perspective.

The afterword–"Inspired Pragmatism in Linfield's Future"–looks ahead to the college as envisioned under the leadership of its newest president, Thomas L. Hellie, and its superb faculty. Here Barbara Seidman offers the perspective of a longtime teacher who has become dean of faculty at an exciting moment in the college's transition to a new century and new educational imperatives.

Sprinkled throughout the narrative the reader will discover vignettes that illuminate three themes highlighted in the current abbreviated mission statement. That motto–"Linfield College: Connecting Learning, Life, and Community "–explicitly reflects Linfield's active, pragmatic heritage. Each vignette tells a story in its own right, helping break up the longer narrative but always, I hope, elucidating and expanding upon it.

I close with a word about photographs and illustrations.

Opposite: *1897-98, Students for the ministry*

Linfield possesses a rich archive of such materials. Together with designers Rob Reynolds and Letha Wulf, Barbara Seidman and I reviewed thousands of images, reducing the number to 180 for this volume. By necessity, to qualify for inclusion, an image had to meet one of two objectives, usually both. It had to advance the narrative or it had to be visually compelling. Unfortunately, many hundreds of images that we could not include also met these criteria. We apologize to readers who conclude that we omitted a favorite image of their own. We plead only that space constraints prompted exclusions that we ourselves lament, knowing firsthand the richness left behind.

Acknowledgments

I thank, first and foremost, Dr. Barbara Kitt Seidman, who served as editor to my drafts and consulted on the book design.

Thanks to Ross Eberman of Carpe Diem Books for proposing four years ago that a sesquicentennial Linfield history would soon be needed. Thanks, too, to book designers Rob Reynolds and Letha Wulf, true professionals in every sense. Rob's exquisite contemporary photographs speak for themselves.

I am indebted to Tim Marsh for his especially careful reading of the entire manuscript and to Judy McNally for her astute copyediting. Kelly Bird and Mardi Mileham went to extraordinary lengths to chase down recent photographs.

Space constraints preclude my specifying others' contributions but I thank them all: Mary Margaret Benson, Gordon Bjork, Susan Bjork, Hollin Buck, Peter Buckingham, Vivian Bull, Laura Dedon, Win Dolan, Bev Epeneter, David Groff, Dave Hansen, Debbie Harmon, David Haugeberg, Thomas Hellie, Laurie Henberg, Katherine Huit, Glenna Kruger, Bill Mackie, Gerald Painter, Jonathan Pierce, Peter Richardson, Eleanor Semon, Jennifer Sokol Blosser, Meridith Symons, Charles Walker, Pam Wheeler, Susan Whyte, and Bruce Wyatt.

Finally, I thank the Executive Committee of the Linfield College Board of Trustees. They ceded me full authorial control over this volume's content. With freedom comes responsibility, so I alone must answer for any errors or omissions. Also, despite the trustees' copyright of these materials, I am solely responsible for all matters of interpretation.

The Story Retold

The title of Linfield's scholarly history, *Bricks Without Straw* (1938), underscores the precariousness of the college's beginnings. Its author, Dr. Jonas A. "Steine" Jonasson, observes early on, "The outlook was dark indeed, for men were trying to make bricks without straw." The biblical reference underlying his title derives from the fifth verse of Exodus, where Pharaoh commands his taskmasters to withhold straw from the Hebrew slaves for their manufacture of bricks. Denying this essential ingredient dramatically increased the workers' labor, because they now had to gather the necessary straw. Although maintaining Jonasson's metaphor might imply an undue pessimism about the college's foundations and fortunes, in fact, Jonasson did not intend his analogy to be either so literal or so bleak. Rather, he meant to emphasize the monumental task undertaken by Linfield's founders. Given the scarcity of essential resources, the labor to ensure Linfield's stability over time has required extraordinary dedication over many generations. The abiding story that is Linfield College derives from a passionate commitment of those who have created and sustained it over the decades. Redoubtable men and women of every era have labored, often beyond reason, to build, preserve, rescue, and advance Linfield. Long hours and tireless effort have provided its main endowment. Given its mission to serve students of modest means, the college has enjoyed scant margin for error.

It remains all the more striking that the college has flourished despite its slender financial base. Combining inspiration with pragmatism, it reaches its sesquicentennial in more robust condition than ever. Today, Linfield's men and women make bricks *with* straw, though the supply continues to be far from lavish and the gathering of it remains a challenge.

Founding

Let us return to the founding. In 1844, Ezra Fisher and Hezekiah Johnson earned appointment as missionaries to the Oregon Territory by the American Baptist Home Mission Society. Fisher had assisted in founding Franklin College in Indiana and Johnson in founding Denison College in Ohio.

Loosely confederated in 1848 into the Willamette Association, the early ranks of Oregon Baptists stayed small. Their first educational effort was to found a primary school near Oregon City, with Johnson's niece as teacher. Fisher, having left Oregon for a time to minister in the California gold fields, found on his return a letter from the Home Mission Society urging establishment of a college. While few of the then eighty-seven Baptists of the association saw immediate need for such a project, Fisher and Johnson prompted them to take the long view. Much as a miner stakes what claim he can without knowing whether ore will be found, Fisher in 1849 formed the Oregon Baptist Education Society to pursue denominational interests.

Opposite: *1890s, Pioneer Hall from the east with water tower and boardwalk*

27

Rev. Hezekiah Johnson and Eliza Shepard Johnson
Oregon Historical Society CN 015867

The society soon sent a resource of a different order in the person of Rev. George C. Chandler, a seven-year president of Franklin College and, prior to that, pastor of the First Baptist Church of Indianapolis. A graduate of Newton Theological Seminary, Chandler had already experienced the ways of the West. His arrival in 1851 roughly coincided with the erection of a building—not paid for—on the fifty-acre site secured by Fisher and Johnson. But Chandler's experience at Franklin made it unlikely he would find much satisfaction in teaching at a primary school, and after little more than a year, he left the presidency of the optimistically named Oregon City College. Importantly for the future, he settled on his own federal land grant just south of Oregon City, where he preached to the local Baptist congregation.

Under the leadership of Professor J.D. Post, the school in Oregon City prospered for a time, though Post drew criticism from the trustees for, among other things, taking "females as scholars." The trustees incorporated in 1856, ambitiously changing the name to Oregon City University. Even so, their schism with Post introduced competition, for he broke away to establish his own school only two miles away. As a functioning entity, Oregon City University ceased to exist, done in by a convergence of factors: a distant sponsoring organization insensitive to frontier conditions, lack of local support, and infighting between trustees and president.

Amidst the jockeying personalities, the idea persisted of securing a Baptist college for the territory. Perhaps the Oregon City project could be revived; if not, perhaps another place would serve just as well. Denominational pride and hope that a college would unify its members led the Willamette Association in 1855 to appoint Fisher and five others to assess the merits of sites in Oregon City, Lafayette, Cincinnati (in the Eola Hills), Santiam, Albany, and Corvallis (at that time the territorial capital).

Ultimately, however, activities in McMinnville with no initial connection to the Baptists superseded the efforts at all other sites. William T. Newby, one of the original six settlers to arrive in Yamhill County in 1844, joined with Sebastian

Even so, the Oregon City site remained insecure from inception to closing—all in less than a decade. Baptists to the south sought to locate the college on the Calapooya River, near present-day Albany. Trustees were appointed and Fisher given charge of placing the college farther south. This plan shortly gave way to a fresh site in Oregon City, which had at least a minimal population. Although Fisher and Johnson put their own resources into securing a land grant of fifty acres near Oregon City, funds were not available to build on it. Throughout 1849, primary instruction took place in a Baptist meeting house in town, with tuition and donations from the Baptist Home Mission Society barely covering operating costs.

Rev. George C. Chandler, first president, 1858 to 1860, Baptist College at McMinnville Oregon Historical Society CN 015924

Adams, who arrived in 1850, to promote plats of land along the Yamhill River. The pair surmised that a local high school might attract buyers. Adams championed a schoolmaster's agenda, with Newby seeking to profit not only from land sales but also from proceeds of his gristmill (an enterprise powered by water diverted from Baker Creek through a mill-race). In 1855 Newby donated five acres for the erection of a school building that was funded by local subscription. Unfortunately, the scale of the building–two wings in an L-shape, each seventy feet long–proved too large for its constituency and too burdensome for either the high school or its McMinnville College successor to maintain adequately.

Believing that their venture required a denominational affiliation, Newby and Adams offered the high school to their own Christian Church. The Christians, however, remained preoccupied with establishing schools at Bethel and Monmouth. They either did not accept the offer of the McMinnville school or temporized so as to make clear their reluctance. Newby and Adams then cast their net wider. They picked up on the publicity generated by the Baptists' search for a new location, and in June 1856, Adams presented an offer at a meeting of the Willamette Association in Santiam. Fisher's site-selection committee thus added McMinnville to its list, and in September declared in its favor.

This decision produced two immediate outcomes. First, the Baptists succeeded in a subscription drive to raise $3,600 to complete the building begun by Adams and Newby. Second, John Wesley Johnson agreed to teach at the school in fall and winter 1857. Johnson later became the second president of McMinnville College, as well as the first president of the University of Oregon.

On January 19, 1858–eleven days before the territorial legislature chartered The Baptist College at McMinnville– William T. and Sarah L. Newby formally transferred ten acres of land, including the L-shaped building, to the trustees of the college. One notable condition, easily endorsed by the Baptists, demanded that title revert to the local school district if college premises ever featured alcoholic beverages, either for sale or for "giving away." Present-day Linfield College no longer occupies the original Newby plat (now the site of McMinnville's First Baptist Church), a detail that saves it from violating this original prohibition.

The second condition underlying the Newby donation directed the "keeping [of] a College school." Aspiration outstripped reality in this regard, for the college department received no qualified students for many years and produced no graduates for over twenty-five years. The charter's scope did sufficiently revive Rev. George Chandler's interest in the earlier Oregon City project to prompt his acceptance of the presidency of The Baptist College at McMinnville. Here

Chandler would not be responsible for the primary school, as that duty fell to George Russell. Initial enrollment permitted him to hire two instructors: C.H. Mattoon and J.D. Post, also veterans of the Oregon City venture. Because the public school movement did not gain traction in McMinnville until later, the college received public funding for its noncollegiate instruction until 1875.

Freed from lower-level teaching duties, Chandler had more time to promote the fledging college than he had enjoyed at Oregon City. He exemplified what became a trend among the school's trustees to hire pragmatic presidents who would do whatever the day required to keep things functioning. Chandler, for instance, performed his own share of repair work on the substandard building inherited from Newby and Adams.

Finally the college had a home, standing third in chronological order of chartered colleges in Oregon and fifth on the Pacific Coast. Even so, security did not ensue. Other denominations championed their own colleges, as with the Methodists at Willamette University (chartered in 1853) and the Congregationalists at Pacific University (chartered in 1854). Worse, the regional Baptists did not unite behind their McMinnville venture, which became the charge of a newly organized Central Baptist Association. The Willamette Association continued alternately to favor either Corvallis or Oregon City as prospective centers for Baptist higher learning. With the outbreak of the Civil War, Oregon Baptists fractured into pro- and antislavery contingents, reducing further the prospects for support, as McMinnville College aligned with the antislavery faction. Farther away and later in time (1877), a Baptist academy in Colfax, Washington, provided additional competition for denominational resources and loyalty. Simply put, the local world into which the uncertain college emerged faced very circumscribed possibilities. Students did not pack up and travel by horse or carriage for long distances to secure an education, even if the effort involved relatively few miles by today's standards. Geographical reality thus reinforced parochialism to weaken

McMinnville College's claim on Northwest Baptists. Luckily, local non-Baptists were also disinclined to travel far. McMinnville College drew a fair share of these students, though attracting non-Baptists failed to inspire the college's primary constituency.

In reflecting on the college for its seventy-fifth anniversary celebration, President Leonard Riley divided Linfield's history into thirds of roughly twenty-five years each: the pioneer period, the precarious period, and the prosperous period. The first extends from the founding through occupancy of Pioneer Hall in 1883. The second moves from 1883 into the early years of the Riley administration, which began in 1906 at what remains the college's lowest ebb. His self-identified prosperous period extended from the middle of the Riley administration to its conclusion. The remaining portion of the retold story falls under these three headings.

The Pioneer Period

Conditions endemic to frontier life undermined curricular aspirations at McMinnville College throughout the decades of the 1850s, '60s, and '70s. These decades unfolded in the deteriorating wood-frame building standing on the original Newby land donation. By 1879, President G.J. Burchett described conditions succinctly: "The building would not keep out water when it rained; nor wind when it blew; nor cold when it froze; and worst of all, it would not burn when it took fire." Nor did the equipment inspire much confidence, as Burchett also observed: "We had an ancient air-pump into which you might put a mouse, and pump all day, and he would sit there in perfect comfort and smile at you."

Efforts to achieve financial stability proved as rickety as the original building. During the 1860s the Central Association undertook a heroic effort to wipe out a college debt of $4,436. Unfortunately, no additional funds remained to build an endowment, which became a preoccupation in the early 1870s. One promising idea, at least initially, resulted in a paper sum of $26,000. Spearheaded by trustee C.H. Mattoon and financial agent Reuben C. Hill, the college launched a

John Wesley Johnson, president, Baptist College at McMinnville, 1864 to 1867; later first president, University of Oregon

Rev. Dr. Mark Bailey, president, 1873 to 1876

Left: *Original building housing The Baptist College at McMinnville, torn down in 1893 to make room for McMinnville's First Baptist Church*

sale of scholarships-in-perpetuity for the sum of $500 apiece. Liberal conditions of use applied: the bearer of a scholarship certificate could send one scholar at a time to the college for full coverage of tuition, books, equipment use, and fees. Moreover, the terms for acquiring the certificates proved lax. Holders could use them by paying only the interest on the promised $500 contribution. Given poor existing records from this period, we cannot today tell how many certificates fell to individuals who reneged on their commitment to pay in full. Once a son or daughter finished school, it doubtless proved tempting for a family to default on the principal.

Many of these certificates—those in the hands of trustees and loyal benefactors—brought in their full subscription pledge. Even so, all perpetual scholarship funds went to cover current expenses rather than to build an investment fund. By the end of the 1870s, "Old Mac" still lacked an endowment and had again fallen into debt to the tune of $3,975. Its obligation to two distinct student groups with differing profiles further compromised institutional aspirations. The first group—perpetual scholarship holders—proved a drain on the tuition of others because inflationary costs lacked buttressing by endowment earnings. The second group consisted of primary and secondary students who, though supporting the institution through their fees or public subsidy, defeated the faculty's ambition to teach at the collegiate level.

Two presidents deserve mention from this period. John

Rev. G.J. Burchett, president, 1878 to 1881, raised the funds to build Pioneer Hall.

Rev. E.C. Anderson, president, 1881 to 1887

Wesley Johnson, who had initially taught at the school in 1857, returned from Yale University to assume the presidency in 1864. He succeeded so well at building student numbers in the primary and secondary departments that in 1866 the trustees leased him the school for five years, in exchange for a commitment that he put $1,000 a year into building maintenance. The college became briefly debt free in Johnson's capable entrepreneurial hands but the interlude ended when he left for Portland in 1867 to become an elementary school teacher.

Johnson's administrative successor remains a mystery. From 1867 until 1873, when the name of Mark Bailey appears in the first extant catalog as "President and Professor of Intellectual and Moral Philosophy and Languages," the college seems to have operated without a president most of the time, save for a four-month term allotted to J.D. Robb. The trustees presumably soldiered on through desultory fund-raising, and those faculty members still employed presumably persevered as teachers at the primary and secondary levels.

President Bailey, a graduate of Rhode Island's Brown University, came to McMinnville from teaching stints at Franklin and at Denison, and from two years' service as president of California College, predecessor to the University of California at Berkeley. His presidency offers the first direct evidence of an emergent collegiate curriculum notable for its ambitious classical foundation. An intellectual of the first order and a man of gentle force, Bailey accepted the presidency at a time of great optimism inspired by the seeming success of financial agent Hill's endowment building. Salaries, including that of the president, grew. Student enrollment remained promising. Within the year, however, the college could not cover costs. Debt accumulated, including unpaid salary owed to President Bailey. When he left office in 1876 to take a position at the University of Oregon, Bailey petitioned the trustees to mortgage college assets in his name. The trustees refused, though they did mount a collection among themselves to cover a portion of the salary owed him. Despite the awkward circumstances surrounding his

departure, Bailey steered an admirable curricular course and earned the fond regard of his students.

Bailey's sturdy belief in a Christian college founded on classical learning inspired the Central Association in 1876 to call on all regional Baptists to rally behind McMinnville College, with its dedication to the "culture of our rising generation, and the perpetuation of our gospel principles of liberty of conscience and freedom of thought." This explicit statement of foundational principles came at a critical juncture. Not only did it inspire those within the fold already, but it also broadened outreach to regional Baptists. The time proved propitious, as earlier denominational schisms relaxed. The proslavery cause had been defeated with the demise of the Confederacy, and the Willamette Association had abandoned its dream of a nearby rival college. Based on the prospect that McMinnville College could now feasibly aspire to be *The* Baptist College of the Northwest (excepting Eastern Washington's Colfax Academy), the trustees remained hopeful as they sought Bailey's replacement.

Unfortunately, the college had to rebound from more than Hill's failed program of selling perpetual scholarships. Recovery from a nationwide financial panic in 1873 (one cause of Hill's difficulties in raising money) proceeded fitfully, and funds remained scarce. A local McMinnville resident, John Magers, became president for seven months, though the trustees had to borrow money to pay him. The next prospective president, S.B. Morse, who was scheduled to assume his duties in fall 1877 for a proffered salary of $1,500, never appeared—a dismal precedent that repeated itself under even more dire circumstances in 1905. After several failed efforts to patch together instruction for the year, the college closed for spring term 1878. This allowed a focused recruitment effort that led to Rev. G.J. Burchett, pastor of Astoria's Baptist church, who accepted the presidency with three conditions: first, that an assistant be hired who could teach across the curriculum; second, that he alone be allowed to determine the course of study; and third, that a now reduced salary of $1,000 be paid in its entirety by year's end.

Burchett's confidence in prescribing terms to the trustees indicates his positive qualities as a leader. He hired D.C. Latourette, a grandson of Ezra Fisher, as his very capable assistant, drawing on Oregon's pioneer legacy and introducing into the college's history the oft-cited Latourette name (see "Pioneer Scion and Scholar," p. 52). President Burchett also increased student numbers, but not by teaching to every student's fancy. Exerting full control over instruction, he successfully reduced the number of courses offered. His sole expansion of the curriculum, a course in professional bookkeeping, started the college in the direction of business instruction.

With a balanced budget for the first time in years and unity among regional Baptists, Burchett championed a capital campaign to replace the drafty building he had inherited. The trustees initially resisted, for some suspected that Burchett would fail and that they would have to close or move the college. Even with good fiscal news in hand, the trustees and Central Baptist Association explored relocation options, but ultimately concurred with their president that "there was no other city more generous than our own McMinnville."

This view drew reinforcement from a vital contribution of twenty acres by Samuel and Mahala Cozine. Early pioneers who met on the trek west in 1843, the couple married in 1845 and secured a 640-acre tract of land in what later became McMinnville. Reputedly the second Baptist convert in the territory of Oregon, Samuel had ties with the school going back to its Oregon City days, having cofounded the Oregon Baptist Education Society with Ezra Fisher and Hezekiah Johnson in 1849. Cozine made his living as a blacksmith but in 1848 headed for the California gold fields, where he fared better than most and returned home with $6,000. Though "Father Cozine" put his name on the college charter and served as a first-generation trustee, it was Mahala who proved the moving force behind their generosity in 1881. Their gift parcel, which included a sturdy tree soon called "The Old Oak," prompted a matching five-acre donation from the widow of President Chandler.

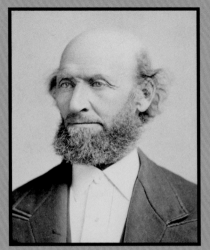

Samuel Cozine

Mahala Cozine

Connecting Community
Community Place Names on Campus

As one might expect, the names of college presidents, deans, faculty members, trustees, and major benefactors regularly adorn the Linfield campus and identify its streets, buildings, and even teaching spaces. A few campus names, however, reflect the contributions of local citizens who served both McMinnville and its college.

First among these stands Pioneer Hall, named to honor the American settlers of Yamhill County and the founders of the college. The pioneer theme continues with Newby Hall, named for William T. Newby, McMinnville's founder and the man who approached regional Baptists to take over the school originally associated with the Christian Church. Cozine Hall pays tribute to Samuel and Mahala Cozine, donors of the land on which Pioneer Hall sits. Campbell Hall recognizes one of the first five settler families in McMinnville.

Mac Hall deliberately recalls the former McMinnville College and the town for which it was named. McMinnville resident Sena Cook provided the funding for Cook Hall in honor of her husband, James H. Cook, class of 1890 and longtime local physician. The building opened in 1945 and originally served as an infirmary. Michelbook House preserves the family name it bore before its move across town in 1992 to become Linfield's Office of Admissions.

By far the most complicated exercise in naming, however, involves Miller Hall, named for three individuals who together epitomize the close town-gown ties between college and community. Not to be confused with the Miller Fine Arts Building (named much later for benefactor James F. Miller), Miller Hall resulted from a trustee motion passed on October 29, 1960.

VOTED: To name and dedicate the new women's dormitory Miller Hall, in honor of three Millers who played significant roles in the development of Linfield College:

Richard Miller, early pioneer minister, one of the first seven incorporators of the Baptist College at McMinnville, and its first treasurer;

Irving E. Miller, brilliant scholar, author and teacher and for thirty-three years a member of the Board of Trustees, contributing much to the curriculum, faculty and presidents of Linfield College;

Dwight Miller, builder of most of the structures on the campus, and a devotee of the College.

1892, Official warranty deed recording transfer of the Cozine land to McMinnville College. Deeds often went unrecorded for years after the actual transaction, which in this case had occurred in 1881.

Right: *Pioneer Hall*

A new president–Rev. E.C. Anderson–oversaw the groundbreaking for the new building on May 31, 1882. Burchett had met Anderson on a fund-raising foray in the East. Despite securing $20,000 for the structure, Burchett had subsequently tendered his resignation, apparently believing that he lacked the confidence of board president A.J. Hunsaker. He did attend the Pioneer Hall dedication on June 12, 1883. Sources differ on the building's total cost, but the figure of $25,000, including equipment, will suffice. William Newby provided bricks at $4.99 per thousand and, like many generous McMinnville business leaders before and since, supplemented his contract with in-kind donations of time and labor. During the dedication ceremony, a dissolving Oregon Baptist Education Society contributed $1,000 from the sale of its original Oregon City property. The very naming of the hall celebrated the commitment of all those constituencies and individuals who over several decades had brought it into being, including Cozine, Newby, and Chandler.

The Precarious Period

Well-constructed in the form of a Greek cross, Pioneer Hall provided ample space for the institution's modest ambitions but proved Spartan in other respects. It housed everything, including the college's scant library, poorly equipped science labs, and minimally furnished class and society rooms. Students renting quarters in the building could purchase firewood or chop it themselves. While the new building gave the struggling college a welcome swagger, it did not solve the underlying difficulties of too few students covering too many costs. In particular, the opening of Pioneer Hall coincided with provision of free public education in McMinnville. An era of friction between the college and the local school district began, ameliorated somewhat in 1889 when the trustees voted to abolish the primary department but unresolved fully until the college abandoned all effort at preparatory education in 1907.

J.H. Smith, later a prominent attorney in Astoria, became McMinnville College's first graduate in 1884, but celebration

1884-1900, Biology lab in Pioneer Hall

of this milestone proved short-lived when the trustees resolved to close the college for fall term 1886 unless $600 could be raised. A.C. Chandler, son of the first president and now a trustee in his own right, provided the final thirty dollars, but only on the evening before term began, with the trustees poised to cancel the session. Such cliffhangers took their toll on the health of President Anderson, who lost sight in one eye due to overexertion. Though he had labored mightily to keep the doors open, he was nonetheless forced to resign. Despite that outcome, Dr. R.E. Storey, professor of English and author of *Linfield Floss and Fiber*, described Anderson fondly: "Always urbane and well groomed in clerical coat and tie, truly classical in poise, he won friends wherever he went."

BAPTIST COLLEGE, McMINNVILLE, OR.

RESOLUTIONS

WHEREAS

DEAN EMERITUS EMANUEL NORTHUP has been called to the great Home-Coming, and we thereby are deprived of a brother in the fellowship of life and of labor, now therefore, be it

RESOLVED by the FACULTY of LINFIELD COLLEGE

THAT in DEAN NORTHUP we have had a fellow-laborer who proved himself at all times a willing and generous bearer of common burdens, and a kindly support and shield to others in bearing their burdens. That in him was a counselor to face difficulties; a friend to share the toils of labor and to participate in the joys of achievement; a guardian of hope to straighten the perplexed path by his word of wisdom born of his experience and his response to the will of God.

THAT the example of DEAN NORTHUP in his wholesome outlook upon this life and his devotion to its tasks; in his faithful, consecrated, and joyous entrance into the ministry of work and continuance therein;

in his faith as laboring ever under the great Taskmaster's eye --- in all these, and in untold other ways, his example shall be for our inspiration, strength, and faithfulness in the common work which he so nobly wrought and which we would carry on.

THAT with profound gratitude we bear our thanks to that kind PROVIDENCE who for these many years so graciously spared to the college and to his fellow teachers and officers such a boon --- the presence in our midst of the man --- DEAN EMANUEL NORTHUP.

THAT we extend to Mrs. Northup and to her family, in their bereavement and sorrow, our Christian sympathy knowing that the qualities of the life of DEAN NORTHUP, which flowed out alike upon the home and the college, and extended wherever he was known, will remain to comfort and solace in sorrow.

BE IT FURTHER RESOLVED

THAT a copy of these resolutions be spread upon the minutes of the Faculty of Linfield College; and that a copy also be presented to Mrs. Northup and her family.

Blanche A. Anderson
PRESIDENT

Ralph E. Storey

Geo. W. Payne
SECRETARY

J. A. Jonasson
COMMITTEE

Adopted by the Faculty of Linfield College · January 12, 1933

In Rev. Truman G. Brownson, Anderson's successor, and in Brownson's first hire, Rev. Emanuel Northup, McMinnville College found a pair of skilled administrators and beloved teachers who not only staved off collapse but transformed the institution into a genuine college. Until Brownson's arrival in 1887 and Northup's in 1888, "Old Mac" had existed as a college more in name than in reality, as the paucity of graduates testifies. An ambitious classical curriculum had been constructed but was offered only one-on-one to a few advanced students such as J.H. Smith. President Brownson, a graduate of Madison University and Baptist Union Theological Seminary, possessed enormous energy and ambition, proving as physically robust as his predecessor had been frail. Like so many of the college's successful presidents, Brownson began with frugality at home. Among his first moves, he cut his own salary from $1,200 to $950. He went on to reduce all other salaries by the same 20 percent, prompting the principal of the academic department, A.J. Crawford, to resign. To fill this crucial slot, now paying a slender $650 a year, he recruited Rev. Emanuel Northup.

Fewer than two in ten colleges founded in America before the Civil War survive today. McMinnville College would in all likelihood have joined that majority had it not been for Northup, the kind of long-serving, much-beloved

Left: *January 12, 1933, Faculty memorial tribute to Dean Emanuel Northup*

Opposite: *1894, President Truman G. Brownson,* left front, *and Dean Emanuel Northup,* right front, *flank the college sign in this community photograph.*

Isabel Grover

Connecting Learning
The Belle of "Old Mac"

Alumna Isabel Margaret Grover (1874–1919) seldom strayed far from her alma mater, returning as a faculty member whose influence extended across generations. Upon her sudden death at age forty-four, Kenneth Scott Latourette, one of her earliest students, penned a moving twenty-page tribute in which he noted: "As a devoted teacher, keen of mind, large of heart, charming in social intercourse, a valued friend and confidant, she is gratefully and affectionately remembered by the scores who passed through her class room and affectionately remembered by the other scores who, while never under her direct tuition, shared the generous hospitality of her home and her heart."

Grover learned to manage adversity early in life. At age nine she "fell through onto a hard floor and both dislocated and broke her hip." Because the injury never healed, she suffered recurrent pain and ill heath. Nonetheless, "Belle" (as she was known then) attended McMinnville College and graduated in 1896. Initially she taught both Latin and art, but after a stint at the University of Chicago, she returned to McMinnville to teach Latin only. Eventually she gravitated to history, the discipline in which she remained for the rest of her career. In another example of faculty assuming multiple roles at the college, she also became the first recorded librarian and first dean of women. She exerted her most enduring influences as a counselor and lifelong correspondent: "To literally hundreds her study and her room at the college were a confessional."

Grover bore the college's troubles at the turn of the century steadfastly committed to its future. A striking example of inspired pragmatism, she handled many long months without a paycheck by organizing students to plant a garden whose harvest might keep her fed and help them pay tuition. While such profits never materialized, the effort did bolster the spirits of the participants.

In another telling example of Grover's focus on students rather than herself, she wrote one graduate to implore that he send money to another who had asked for a loan. Though she had not been paid in months, she promised to retire the debt immediately on receiving her next paycheck. The two-tiered exchange occurred, with both loans subsequently repaid.

At Isabel Grover's death, President Leonard Riley declared in his annual report: "Inasmuch as she builded herself so vitally into the history of McMinnville College, some suitable memorial of her should be provided for, and my own suggestion is that one of the buildings of the girls' group in our new plan be called 'Isabel M. Grover Hall.'"

teacher and caretaker whose dedicated service typified the institutions that remain. Arriving in McMinnville at age thirty-seven as professor of mathematics, "Old Baldy" (as four decades of graduates came to know him) had himself graduated from Colgate University in upstate New York and later entered the University of Chicago's divinity school. Given such credentials, he received a rude shock upon finding only seven of the roughly one hundred students qualified to study at the undergraduate level. McMinnville delivered its own set of surprises: except for a few planked walkways in the business district, "the streets were bottomless pits when wet and oceans of dust when dry." Recalling these discoveries some twenty-five years later, Northup conceded, "I had never seen a more desolate looking place in my life."

Because Brownson and Northup both believed that only denominational support could secure the college's future, they helped bring into being the Oregon State Baptist Convention. With Brownson serving as its first president, the convention quickly assumed statewide responsibility for the college. Although this organizational support proved beneficial in the end, initially it undermined the college's local base, for Brownson campaigned for a move to Portland, where more Baptists resided and the community still lacked higher education options. The trustees agreed on condition that $150,000 be raised in Portland to provide an endowment and demonstrate serious commitment to the project.

When Portland funding failed to materialize, Brownson and Northup successfully maintained both Baptist and McMinnville support for the college and their vision for its future in the Yamhill Valley. In 1889 the Oregon Convention produced $1,730 to complete a $10,000 fund-raising drive to which Portland banker Josiah Failing had pledged a matching grant of $5,000. The Failing Fund became the first permanent endowment at the college. All previous campaign dollars had gone either to support capital projects or to reduce accumulated debts.

The Brownson-Northup partnership produced a number of milestone events: campus chapters of the Young Men's

Christian Association (YMCA) and Young Women's Christian Association (YWCA) opened; *The Review* began publication; literary societies and athletic clubs were founded; public examinations before a trustee board of visitors were initiated; the number of years required for a degree shrank from four to three; and Northup inaugurated the first required course bearing directly on the college's Christian mission, "Church History and Homiletics," a class he taught over four decades. That it took so long to establish these features of a residential Christian college speaks to the continuing precariousness of the institution. The course on homiletics also exposed an unresolved debate among Baptists on how best to ensure the school's Christian identity. Some partisans held that the college should hire its president and key faculty from the ministry and require daily chapel (leaving Bible instruction to local congregations, which all faculty and students were presumed to join). Others held that the college ought to adopt a specifically theological curriculum, emphasizing preministerial training for all. Realistically, McMinnville College had insufficient resources until the 1890s—either in dollars or in qualified students—for the debate in favor of theological instruction to gain much traction. Under Brownson and Northup, Baptist commitment in life and in learning became inextricably linked. Even though not a center within the curriculum, religious devotion permeated the college environment, as evidenced by the choice of its first woman graduate, Ida Skinner (class of 1891), to enter overseas missionary work.

The first substantial picture of student life emerges thanks to Brownson's establishment of *The Review* in 1895. Brownson served as editor in chief and established the publication to address the interests not only of the college community, but also of Northwest Baptists and others in the region with literary inclinations. An indefatigable pamphleteer, Brownson produced an organ that bound the community together, promoted the college to its larger constituencies, and served as its administrative mouthpiece.

Early editions of *The Review* contain reflections on Chris-

tian commitment, a sketch of college history by Brownson, and many occasional pieces by current students. One notable author, "Belle Grover," later became the much-loved instructor Isabel Grover (see "The Belle of 'Old Mac,'" p. 38), for whom the college's first women's residence hall was named. *The Review* also provided regular accounts of the activities of the YMCA and YWCA, predecessors of today's student government. Its pages featured competition updates on regional men's sports clubs in football, baseball, track and field, and basketball. Intramural activities such as women's archery, athletics, and basketball failed to gain traction as intercollegiate sports for decades in the face of objections to the public display of women in competition (see "Basketball for Women," p. 42).

In the 1890s, sports of any kind actually took a back seat to events centered on public speaking and debate. After student Charles V. Galloway took first place in the 1896 State Intercollegiate Oratorical Contest, he returned to town to find the president, faculty members, students, and prominent citizens of McMinnville gathered at the train station to cheer his victory and join in a celebratory parade. The student body even prevailed on the college to declare a holiday from classes in favor of a program of impromptu public speaking. Such priorities led C.W. Converse to publish, in the first volume of *The Review,* a subtle rebuke: "McMinnville College has already won deserved rank among the leading colleges of the state in oratory; in the near future let us make her such in the noble field of athletics."

The public acclaim given Galloway's success underscores the curricular pride of place accorded "elocution" at a college chartered in the same year as the Lincoln-Douglas debates. Before radio nationalized public discourse, the unamplified spoken word held both local and practical importance at entertainment venues. Some of the first nonchurch connections between town and gown often came in the form of Friday night debates and oratorical contests that attracted many McMinnville residents to campus. The college's 1872-73 catalog signals the priority given to public

Rev. T.G. Brownson, president, 1887 to 1896

Rev. Harry L. Boardman, president, 1896 to 1903

A.M. Brumback, president, 1903 to 1905, wife Clara, and daughter Alma

speaking in its listing of Miss Anna Bean as "Professor of Natural Sciences and Elocution," an unusual combination of disciplines by today's standards but one taken for granted at the time. The college's first literary club, the Philergian Society, organized in 1874, provided a forum for skilled discourse and written composition and served as a forerunner of latter day social clubs, service clubs, and Greek-letter fraternities and sororities (see "Going National," p. 83).

Alcohol and tobacco remained strictly banned, as did student appearances in public dance halls, billiard parlors, and skating rinks. Occasionally, the faculty proved too zealous in its prosecution of these strictures, leading the trustees to reduce a punishment deemed excessive. While the expressed standards themselves stood unchallenged, such trustee action served as a reminder that young people deserved some flexibility from the adults charged with their character formation.

When Brownson left to head California College in 1896, the trustees hired as president Rev. Harry L. Boardman, pastor of the First Baptist Church in Eugene. Boardman had studied at McMinnville, then at Colfax College and the University of Chicago. He came to lead a college that had witnessed some significant gains under Brownson's tenure:

the assets provided by the Failing Fund; a doubling of tuition revenues in the first half of the 1890s; a successful expansion into music instruction (see "The Conservatory," p. 66); acquisition of a second campus building, the Observatory, with its fine new telescope; and a handsome expansion of the library. Still, the aftermath of a major financial panic in 1893 brought the familiar fiscal wolf to the doors of the entire community, with the next ten years proving the darkest in college history.

President Boardman's conscientious reports to the trustees offer an affecting glimpse into a self-doubting man who loved the college but felt unequal to the challenge of keeping it solvent. He chides himself for his fiscal deficiencies but then agrees with those trustees who argue that fund-raising duties best belong to a "financial agent" and not to a president. He tendered his resignation early, only to be persuaded by the board to remain in office. When he finally yielded in 1903 to Professor A.M. Brumback, head of the science department, the college had fallen into habits of serious financial irresponsibility. Among them, the mortgaging of college assets meant that interest income went toward the mortgages rather than the operating budget. President Brumback, an athletics enthusiast who as a faculty member had briefly played center for the football team, proved even less able to reverse the college's financial straits. Once again teachers went unpaid as the college issued warrants in lieu of cash. Local merchants accepted the warrants at a discount, knowing they risked never being paid. Though the McMinnville citizenry had often enough helped rescue the college by responding to its solicitations and providing in-kind services, the warrants added a new and mutually unwelcome dimension to town's subsidy of gown. Still, merchants steadfastly honored them and even extended credit to penurious students.

Unable to stem a tide of accumulating debt and uncollected income, Brumback resigned in 1905, with grim results. Twice the trustees believed they had hired a new president: each time the candidate accepted the offer but declined to assume office on the date anticipated. Emanuel Northup

1903-04, College debate league champions. Bottom to top: *Kenneth Scott Latourette, J. Bradford Dodson, Walter Dyke (Sr.)*

Opposite: *1890s, Women's athletics class*

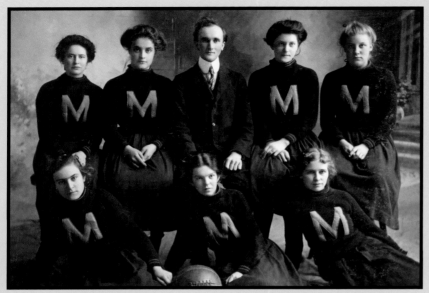

1901-02, Women's basketball team

Connecting Learning
Basketball for Women

Until the 1950s, Linfield women engaged in sports either as intramural activity or on designated "Sports Days" and "Play Days" arranged with rival colleges. Attitudes toward women's competition vacillated between grudging recognition of the benefits of moderate exercise and objections to women's performance before male viewers. The following exchange between President W.N. Ferrin of Pacific University and President A.M. Brumback of Linfield typifies this ambivalence.

January 19, 1905
My dear President Brumback:—
Wont (sic) you give me your views touching the playing of Basket-Ball (sic) games away from home by girls. Our Dean of Women is strongly opposed to the practice, but the instructor and the girls are quite "fierce" to be allowed to have games with your girls and others. Do you fully approve, or do you give your consent a sort of protest (sic)? Do you favor in such games the admission of a promiscuous audience; or if not what restrictions do you favor placing upon the attendance? I shall be glad to have your views as soon as convenient.

January 20, 1905
My Dear Sir:—
Yours of recent date with reference to basket ball (sic) by women is received. If you desire my own very private opinion in the matter I must admit that I do not favor basket ball for women at all. As far as the exercise is concerned, I consider the game every whit as violent as foot ball (sic) and therefore far too rough for the great majority of girls. I have known girls to go into series of fainting spells after a game. As far as the ethical and aesthetic side of it is concerned, I dread to have the day come when my girl will show herself willing to become the public target for the eyes and voices of the lot of howling hoodlums who usually gain admittance with respectable people, just to see the girls play.

Women's basketball attire consisted of "girdles to furnish garters to hold up our long black stockings over which we wore full, pleated wool serge bloomers and heavy black middy blouses with big ties." Given President Brumback's caveat about impropriety, the college forbade men's attendance, though in 1909, "three 'villains,' namely George Stewart, Art Larsell, and Paul Breuning, sneaked in wearing girl's clothes and watched the game from the stands."

agreed to become acting president while the trustees made futile offers to two additional prospects, including ex-President Boardman. Dr. Jonasson aptly sums up this bleakest phase of college history:

> By the end of 1905 the presidency of McMinnville College had been refused by four men, and the prospect of getting the right man was darker than ever. No one was willing to try making bricks without straw, when for a half century able and determined men had failed in the attempt. Little wonder that some of the Portland members of the board of trustees decided that if a leader could not be secured soon they would move, at the meeting of the board on January 10, 1906, that the school close its doors in June.

The Prosperous Period

The promise of long-delayed prosperity revived in the person of Rev. Leonard W. Riley, who rose to the challenge of the presidency precisely because no one else would do so. A graduate of Denison University and the Rochester Theological Seminary, Riley found his calling first and foremost in shoring up the Baptist denomination in the Northwest. Perhaps he sought to preclude the insult that would accrue to Oregon Baptists—among whom he stood as an exemplar—if McMinnville College failed.

Riley's first position in the Northwest came in 1901 as pastor of McMinnville's First Baptist Church. The college had literally given birth to the church, providing not only a sanctuary within the building the college had inherited from the Christian Church, but also ministerial support through its presidents and faculty members. Riley's pastoral duties made him familiar to President Boardman and Dean Northup as he worked to efface a $1,700 church debt in six short months. Because the larger denomination needed such leadership, in 1903 he became Oregon missionary for the American Baptist Home Mission Society and secretary of the Oregon State

Opposite: 1904, Required chapel service in Pioneer Hall

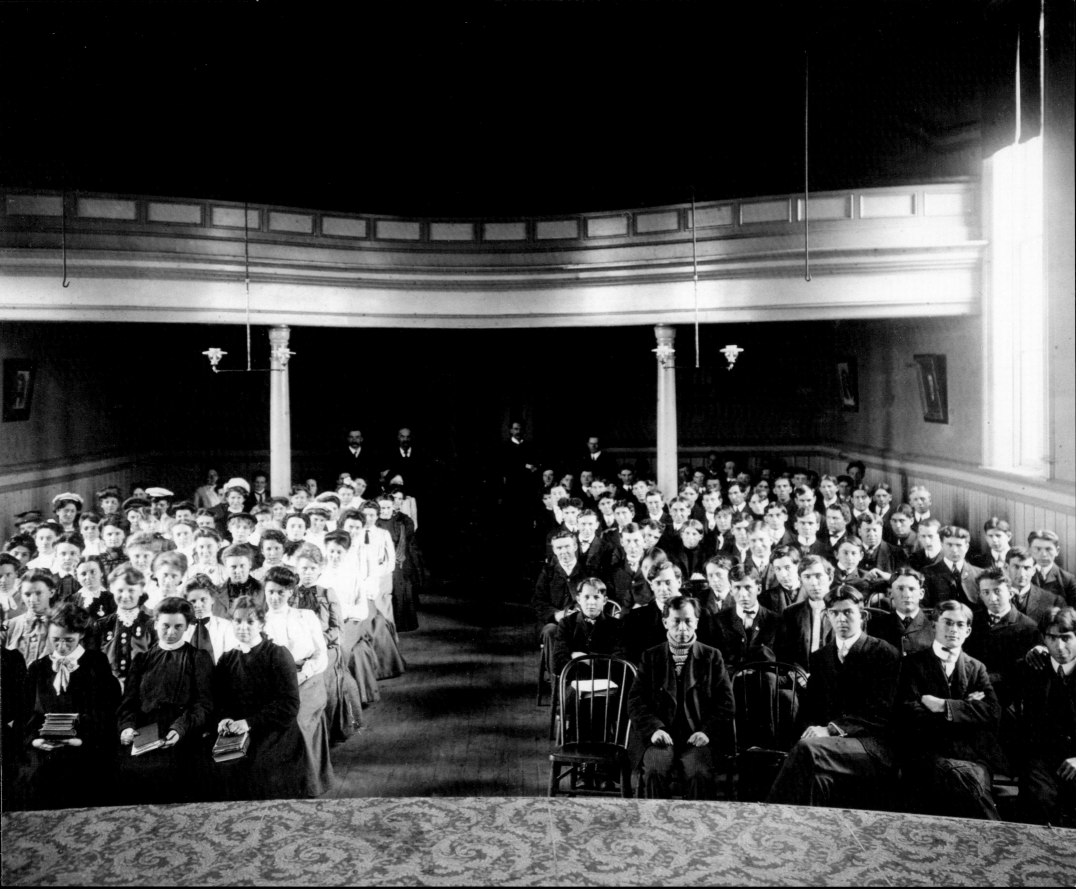

Baptist Convention. In these allied roles, he successfully steered many church constituencies out of debt and into ardent expansion of their mission. In 1906 when he assumed the reins of McMinnville College at age thirty-four, Riley had established a strong reputation within those Baptist communities whose solvency he had bolstered. Their indebtedness to him mirrors today's veteran congressional delegate who raises significant campaign funds for other candidates.

As Burchett had done in the early 1880s, Riley prescribed rigorous terms of acceptance to the trustees, who rejoiced to find someone willing "to pull [the college] out of the hole if he can." First, the college needed to adopt new bylaws, particularly with regard to strengthening the trustees' fiduciary oversight. Second, the board had to make an immediate collective pledge of $1,000. Third, Riley demanded authority to nominate the members of all board committees. He left his own compensation to the board, which voted him a salary of $1,500 a year—the very sum spurned in the 1877 hunt for a president.

Riley entered office as a man on a mission. Two months into his presidency, *The Pacific Baptist* published an extensive illustrated feature on McMinnville College, touting it as deserving, indeed commanding, support from all members. Its author argued that a college with the good fortune to attract Rev. Leonard Riley to its presidency stood at the dawn of a new era. Before long Riley began to justify such claims. He used his appointive powers well, establishing a finance committee of E.C. Apperson, James F. Failing, and W.O. Haynes, men with the connections and clout to assist the crusading young president. Before long Henry Failing's widow and two daughters augmented the Failing Fund by $10,000. Riley set his sights high: $100,000 in subscriptions would efface the institution's burdensome debt, releasing the endowment to subsidize current expenses. In addition, he planned to add $50,000 to that endowment.

In his initial campaign, Riley made significant progress among Washington Baptists, a necessity if McMinnville were to become *The* Baptist College of the Northwest. Riley's pred-

ecessors had downplayed such ambitions, given Baptist respect for local church autonomy and a denominational commitment to freedom of conscience (or "soul freedom") and free association among believers. Pressing the case for McMinnville College meant competing head-to-head with Colfax College and Adelphia College (established by Swedish Baptists in Seattle). Such tactics posed an unsavory challenge to many regional Baptists, who tended toward platitudes encouraging all institutions to prosper according to the rectitude of their common cause. Though diplomatic both in dress and discourse, Riley proved a force of nature in promoting his institution at the expense of the others. His early fund-raising successes for the Oregon State Baptist Convention had taught him that in a realm of scarcity, sufficient financing of one entity would necessarily occur at the expense of others seeking the same support. With allies from

1910, McMinnville College Review staff. Seated center: W. Lester Adams (editor). Others, left to right: Margaret McCloskey, Margaret Campbell, Everett S. Burkett, Frank G. Pettit, F.P. Manley, W.P. Jeffrey

Opposite: 1909, L.L. Sorority members, posing with their heads through pages of the McMinnville Telephone-Register, realize their stated mission "for social improvement and clean, wholesome college fun."

the board and his own earlier contacts, he concluded an agreement directing the bulk of support from Washington Baptists south into Oregon. Adelphia College thus passed out of the hands of the Baptists and, by 1919, became the site of a Catholic preparatory school.

Within the campus proper, Riley did not simply hunker down and wait for better times. While rigorously controlling expenses elsewhere, Riley saw that the college's special and separate tuition for music equaled the tuition earned from the entire remaining academic program. To move conservatory musicians out of Pioneer and into their own space, he began construction of Music Hall, a $7,000 "temporary" building lacking a foundation. He also attended to other improvements in the physical plant. Private fireplaces in classrooms, offices, and living quarters gave way to the college's first central heating plant in 1909, the same year Music Hall opened.

Riley also provided impetus for curricular reform. In 1908 he returned the college to the national norm of requiring four years of undergraduate study to earn a bachelor's degree. The faculty clustered courses into eight different groupings (e.g., classical, Latin-philosophical, scientific, pedagogical), directing students more emphatically toward specific careers or subsequent graduate study. By 1921, the now familiar system of majors and minors had taken root.

Meanwhile Riley accomplished in the national Baptist community what he had accomplished among those in Washington—namely, promoting the cause of higher education (and, by extension, of McMinnville College) to unprecedented levels. He advocated creation of a standing Board of Education for the Northern Baptist Convention that by 1913 produced $60,000 in one-time contributions to McMinnville College. These efforts spawned a revised overall campaign effort with a then-staggering goal of $300,000. In large measure this target figure derived from a

Opposite: *1922, May Queen Jessie M. Jeffrey's court with Professor of English E.S. Gardiner in black cap,* left

1910, May Queen Myrtle Maxwell

1915, May Pole dance, women only

Connecting Life
May Day

Many generations of Linfield alumni recall May Day as one of their signature memories of undergraduate days. Begun in 1904, it proved a ready-made morale-boosting exercise for President Leonard Riley upon his arrival in 1906, when the threat of closure weighed heavily on McMinnville College.

May Day, with its pagan origins and its reliance on children running wildly around a May Pole with streamers flying, seems a contradiction in terms for a Baptist institution headed by a strict adherent to the faith. But President Riley saw value in providing students with a celebratory occasion to anticipate, plan, and enjoy. As a later-day writer for the *Oregon Journal* surmised in 1947, Riley may have had pragmatic motives as well:

> When one delves into the history of the May Day celebration at Linfield, one is apt to form a secret opinion that Dr. Riley was a wise psychologist and figured out an excellent way to achieve a thorough spring cleaning on the college grounds.

May Day occurred on the first Saturday of the month. On the preceding Friday—Campus Day—

"all students, unless specifically excused by the student association, must work at improving the campus and making ready for the May Day program on the following day." In 1947, the fine for not participating had grown to a robust fifty cents.

As the program evolved, the Queen's Bard (for twenty years, Dr. Ralph Storey) celebrated the May Queen in poetry, and the Court Bishop saw to the coronation (Harold Elkinton was a favorite for this office). She then made various proclamations useful to the next year's community. She would, for instance, name the incoming members of the Daughters of Tradition (D.O.T.s) and Intercollegiate Knights—the women's and men's service organizations. She also presided over the Cap and Gown Ceremony, announcing the graduating seniors. Following these serious proclamations came "the burning of the green," at which first-year men threw their green beanies onto the fire and first-year women their green bows.

Through sixty-six consecutive years, Linfield's May Queens reigned, from Queen Bernice I (Bernice Sears) in 1904 to Spring Festival Queen Penny Pease in 1969. The festival disappeared when it seemed no longer relevant to a rising generation preoccupied with the Vietnam War and women's liberation. Attempts to revive the tradition in the mid-1980s led to the naming of May Queens on both the Portland and McMinnville campuses, and even included introduction of a May King. Since traditions emerge, live, and die on their own schedules, the revival effort failed.

Connecting Learning
"Mother" Potter

Born in the same year that McMinnville College received its charter—1858—Carrie Casler Potter became a teacher early in life, taking positions at the Pillsbury Academy (Minnesota), Colgate Theological Seminary (New York), and Bridgeton Institute (New Jersey). After graduating from the New England Conservatory of Music with a bachelor of music degree in 1899, she undertook post-graduate study with choral conductors and composers in New York and Boston. In Chicago, she studied with George Frederick Root, known for his sacred music and world-renowned for his Civil War compositions, including "The Battle Cry of Freedom." Mrs. Potter came to McMinnville College in 1904, one of a trio of "greatest assets" (the others being Isabel Grover and Emanuel Northup) whom Leonard Riley credited with saving the college in its darkest days.

As dean of the conservatory, Mrs. Potter established a tradition of excellence in vocal performance. She simultaneously led the choir at McMinnville's First Baptist Church. Her college-community performing groups raised money for many good causes, as evidenced in a 1920 flyer for *H.M.S. Pinafore*, proceeds going to the public library.

In his funeral tribute to her in June 1947, Dr. William R. Frerichs concluded: "She loved people, she loved her college. Even after her retirement . . . she retained her interest in the college and found constant delight in revisiting the campus to enjoy its progress, to meet old friends and to form new friendships among faculty and students. She kept young by mingling with youth who on their part never failed to admire her inspiring personality."

Formal portrait of Rev. Leonard W. Riley, president, 1906 to 1931, from the 1921 Oak Leaves

presidents of these institutions wrote each other about their progress in raising the sum required to match Hill's pledges. Albany and Willamette eventually collected, but by 1916, when McMinnville College could affirm similar success, Hill had died. His executors chose not to honor the pledge despite repeated appeals from President Riley and Dr. Myron W. Haynes, who had served as the most successful financial agent in college history up to that time. While Hill's pledge had prompted others to contribute on an unprecedented level to the school's welfare, it yielded nothing in its own right. The experience understandably soured Dr. Haynes, who watched as some of his matching pledges evaporated.

Meanwhile, the college also had to contend with the impact of America's entry into World War I on April 6, 1917. The U.S. armed forces enlisted 167 McMinnville College students during the conflict, six of whom died in combat. Enrollment dropped from a high of 263 in 1916-17 to a low of 104 in 1918-19, the vast majority female. Gladys Strong (class of 1919) became the first woman elected president of the Associated Students of McMinnville College. The college sought to boost its male population by initiating a Student Officer Training Corps, but the attempt failed. A general detestation of all things German depleted German language classes led by Professor William R. Frerichs (see "Servant Historians," p. 86), a native of that country. Despite the loss of the Hill pledge, Myron Haynes oversaw a capital campaign successful enough to compensate for this enrollment slump without significant diminution of resources. Equally importantly, Haynes achieved a milestone event in recruiting Frances Ross Linfield to the board of trustees in 1917. A new degree of prosperity lay just around the corner, as did a name change.

Born in 1852 in Penfield, New Jersey, Frances Eleanor Ross earned a BA degree from New York's Elmira College. She then taught high school in Illinois, Pennsylvania, and upstate New York before marrying the Rev. George Fisher Linfield in 1878. George Linfield had graduated from the University of Rochester in 1873 and from its seminary the next

pledge of $50,000 by "Empire Builder" James J. Hill, president of the Great Northern Railroad, on condition that the college secure matching funds totaling $200,000.

Correspondence on the Hill pledge tells a story that, in miniature, reflects the uneven fortunes of the college throughout its hundred and fifty years. Hill had made similar pledges to Albany College, College of Puget Sound, Pacific University, Pacific College, and Willamette University. The

Overleaf: 1917, McMinnville College students training under army Captain Leonard Hopfield (class of 1901) during World War I before leaving for active duty at the end of the semester

Connecting Learning

Pioneer Scion and Scholar

Kenneth Scott Latourette sprang from dedicated educational stock. His father, DeWitt Clinton "D.C." Latourette, served as an early teacher and later treasurer (1892 to 1906) of McMinnville College, and his mother, Ellen Latourette, taught Latin at Pacific University. An uncle, Lyman Latourette, held the position of secretary of McMinnville College (1906 to 1915). A young aunt, Nellie Latourette, actually attended college with Kenneth. The family's lineage went back to Ezra Fisher, pioneer founder of the Oregon Baptist Education Society; Kenneth and Nellie collected and published his letters in 1919.

At the time of Kenneth's 1904 graduation from McMinnville College, most Eastern schools recognized its degree as equivalent to that from a junior college. During a fifteen-month hiatus in his father's Oregon City bank, Kenneth taught himself Greek to qualify for Yale College, where he took his BA in history and earned a Phi Beta Kappa pin in 1906. He went on to earn a doctorate in history from Yale in 1909.

Latourette's 1967 autobiography, *Beyond the Ranges*, provides a vivid picture of the early-twentieth-century struggles that almost closed the doors of McMinnville College. D.C. Latourette underwrote the college's $45,000 debt, which in 1904 had not yet exceeded net college assets of $50,000 but would do so by the time of Kenneth's graduation from Yale. Still, in other ways the college shone: speaking of its faculty, Kenneth Latourette wrote, "I have said that the best teaching I had there was better than the best I had at Yale and the worst teaching I had was not as bad as the worst I had at Yale."

After brief missionary work in China and teaching stints at Reed College and Denison University, Latourette became a member of the Yale faculty in 1921. His seven-volume *History of the Expansion of Christianity* and five-volume *Christianity in a Revolutionary Age* remain seminal works for every serious scholar of the Christian faith. Over the course of his distinguished career he became president of the American Historical Association (1947) and Sterling Professor of Oriental Missions at Yale (1949).

Before his death in 1968, Latourette visited Oregon and Linfield College nearly every year. He took great pride in his alma mater, which had recognized him in various ways across the decades: in 1925 he received the first honorary doctorate bestowed on an alumnus, and in 1967 he became Distinguished Alumnus of the Year. In 1950, the college named Latourette Hall to honor his pioneering family and their contributions to the institution's survival.

DeWitt Clinton Latourette, treasurer, 1892 to 1906

1944, President Harry Dillin, left, with Mrs. and Dr. Olof Larsell flanking Kenneth Scott Latourette, who delivered the inaugural Frank Larsell Memorial Lecture

year. In 1883, the couple moved to Wisconsin, where George served as principal of Wayland Academy until his death in 1890. His widow enrolled in a doctoral program at the University of Chicago in 1894 but curtailed her aspiration the next year in order to care for her ailing parents in Spokane, Washington. Both parents died shortly thereafter, leaving Frances to become a businesswoman and sometime high school teacher in Spokane, where her generous support of the Grace Baptist Church brought her to the attention of Dr. Haynes.

Before long Frances Linfield and Dr. Riley, who had first met in 1908, became friends and confidants. According to *The Review* in 1922, Riley's earnest commitment "to eliminate from student life everything that is inconsistent with the Christian principles" favorably impressed Mrs. Linfield. By 1918 she had told Riley, Board President B.F. Rhodes, and Treasurer Charles Kopf that she and her husband had promised one another that if God ever favored them in a material way, they would dedicate their fortune to Christian education. She now declared that she would make McMinnville College the beneficiary of this pledge, though for nearly four years the terms remained secret. Her Spokane property, valued at between $250,000 and $300,000, would be transferred to the trustees if they would name the institution in honor of her husband.

Because various means of arranging the transfer failed, nothing official occurred immediately. Meanwhile, in 1921 Mrs. Linfield succeeded Carrie Potter (see "'Mother' Potter," p. 48) as dean of women and lived with President Riley and his wife, serving without salary. On January 10, 1922, President Riley disclosed to the full board the terms of the agreement with Mrs. Linfield, and Rev. A.J. Hunsaker elicited a unanimous vote for his motion that the institution's name become Linfield College. Late that afternoon students and faculty were summoned to a chapel meeting to receive the welcome news. The administration declared a class holiday for the following day—a Wednesday—replete with festivities.

Certain details undisclosed in the excitement of the

Leonard Riley on Football

On March 1, 1916, while celebrating his tenth anniversary as president of McMinnville College, Leonard Riley delivered the following judgment on football:

> When I was a lad in the country school there was one game which we played from morning until night, season in and season out. . . . That game was football played in the old-fashioned way when kicking the ball was the main part of the game, and the running involved developed both muscle and lungs. The following year the change was made to the modern method of playing the game. I went out with the rest of the boys and practised (sic) the new methods, and then I said to them: "Boys, you'll have to excuse me; I think too much of my face, my limbs and my life to run the risk of having them ruined in any such game as that."

> What I have seen of the game since that time has but strengthened my conviction that the modern game of football has no more place in a Christian institution, or a civilized country, than has bull baiting and prize fighting. One of the first recommendations I made to the Board of Trustees of McMinnville College was that the game of football as then played should be prohibited. It was unanimously adopted; and Professor Northup, who has been with the College for more than a quarter of a century, insists that few, if any, of the actions of the Board of Trustees during this decade, have done any more for the improvement of the moral tone of the institution than has the elimination of this game with its spirit of rowdyism and brutality. In this respect I have seen another of my ideals of College life in such a way that neither the Trustees nor the Faculty would for one minute consider a reinstatement of the game in McMinnville College.

The emergence of gang tackling had epitomized the "modern methods" Riley deplored, and no doubt he approved when U.S. President Theodore Roosevelt in 1906 demanded rule changes that eliminated the practice. Such

reforms bolstered the game's image over time and led boosters among McMinnville College's male student body to lobby regularly for football's reinstatement. They won the day with an announcement to that effect at chapel on January 10, 1922. Right on its heels came even better news: the announcement of Frances Ross Linfield's bequest and the college's imminent name change.

Given conditions at the college in 1922, the opponents of football, including Riley, might have lamented its cost as much as its morality. Still, in Riley's defense, Roosevelt's reforms had eliminated much "rowdyism and brutality" from the game.

1904, McMinnville College football team. Back rows, left to right: *Roy Calavan, W. Lair Thompson (coach), Corwin McKee (manager), unidentified.* Middle row, left to right: *unidentified, unidentified, Bill Elmore, Bennie Linderman, unidentified, Leonard Hopfield.* Seated, left to right: *Roy Hill, Claude Calavan, Floyd Patty (captain), Eugene Cramer, George B. Day, Fred H. Thompson.* Players mentioned in game reports and so possibly pictured: *Clifford Gray, Bela Gowen, Lewis Miller, Arthur Phillips, James Ward.*

Rev. Andrew Jackson Hunsaker, trustee from 1866 until his death in 1923 and three times Board of Trustees president: 1871 to 1882, 1885 to 1889, and 1889 to 1905

moment made the gift more problematic than it initially appeared. One complication involved controversy over the sources of the Linfield fortune. The official story stated that Mrs. Linfield's assets stemmed entirely from the pact she had made with her husband and from an ensuing frugality that led them to bank the whole of her salary one year and the whole of his salary the next. She perhaps championed this official version because it made her husband's contribution to the gift seem larger than it had been in fact. No doubt thrift provided one source of the wealth she shared with the college, but this account omits other sources.

First, one must acknowledge the role of Frances Linfield's parents, who, according to the Spokane auditor's office, deeded property to her in 1894 in exchange for her assumption of liability for back taxes. Though she accepted such risk during a national recession, she also acquired the property on very favorable terms. This acquisition underscores a second factor informing Mrs. Linfield's wealth —namely, her astute business sense. From 1894 until well after the gift of property to McMinnville College, Spokane County records show her selling and acquiring property on a regular basis. She fared better than most and as well as all but a handful of local real estate moguls. Whatever initial nest egg she and her husband had set aside in the cause of Christian education stood dwarfed by the appreciated value of her property in Spokane. Moreover, all of her significant acquisitions came during her widowhood.

A final and later highly contentious source of the Linfield fortune (see "Contesting a Legacy," p. 89) involved her brother, Edward Sherman Ross, her cotrustee in the Ross Holding Company. Edward died in 1915, and in 1916 a key asset of the holding company was transferred to Frances Linfield "in consideration of the sum of Seventy-five Thousand ($75,000) Dollars." This acquisition became the most valuable parcel within her gift to the college. Some in the Ross family believed that this property had been given to Frances Linfield "in trust," a pact allegedly violated by her bequest. The Spokane auditor's records, however, verify that title had

Rev. George Fisher Linfield, circa 1870s-90s

indeed been conveyed to her alone, without restrictions.

In another undisclosed term of the gift, its full value did not accrue to the institution when it received title to the Spokane properties. Mrs. Linfield continued to draw an annuity equivalent to approximately half the earnings from the real estate until subsequent sale of some properties allowed investment of the proceeds to cover the annuity until her death. Because management of the properties required a significant commitment from college officials and from Frances Linfield herself, she also received a small stipend. Nor did the property always provide a predictable return. After she took up permanent residence in McMinnville, some tenants in Spokane exploited their absentee

1930, Front view of Melrose Hall when newly completed

Connecting Community
Treat's Treat

Only one year after the announcement of Mrs. Linfield's gift, a benefactor who insisted on anonymity stepped forward to give President Leonard Riley 10,000 shares of Penn-Mex Fuel stock. Riley was advised to put the shares in a lockbox and forget about them until they appreciated to $40 a share (from a present value of $17). In 1928, they sold collectively for $383,000.

President Riley urged the donor family and its representatives to permit him to recognize them publicly, but M.C. Treat of Pennsylvania, source of the largesse, steadfastly declined. His sole concession involved the naming of the building erected with a portion of his money after one of his favorite spots on earth. Thus Scotland's Melrose Abbey produced an unlikely namesake in Linfield's Melrose Hall.

The story does not end here. When M.C. Treat's widow died in Pomona, California, in 1934, her son and Linfield alumnus Gordon Palmer transmitted a second significant gift of $60,000 to the college. President Elam Anderson, who recalled a Melrose Hall made possible by a similar Treat bequest to the University of Shanghai, again asked permission to name a building at Linfield in honor of the family. He specifically proposed naming the new women's dormitory in honor of Mrs. Treat. When the family again refused permission, the building became Failing Hall instead.

To this day the Treats' considerable generosity goes without explicit public commemoration at Linfield, except in this volume.

Rev. John B. Champion

Connecting Learning
Champion's Campaign

"I came [to McMinnville from Philadelphia in 1914] misled by the same innocent faith shared by so many that because the President, who teaches nothing, is conservative, the teaching of the School is conservative."

So runs one sentence in a lengthy May 1917 complaint to the trustees against three faculty members at McMinnville College. The letter identified its targets as J. Sherman Wallace, professor of public speaking and Bible; F.G. Boughton, professor of philosophy and French; and Isabel M. Grover, professor of history. Rev. John B. Champion, pastor of McMinnville's First Baptist Church, charged that these three embraced liberal theology, naturalism, evolution, and a pernicious doctrine "in ethics that conscience is an authority superior to that of the Bible."

Students and colleagues alike voiced support for the three faculty members. For his part, President Leonard Riley had already made clear his differences with Boughton by confiscating one of his textbooks and ordering a change of syllabus earlier that spring. Boughton left over the summer for Denison University, where late in his career he taught Winthrop Dolan, subsequently dean of faculty and twice acting president of Linfield. Wallace and Grover, however, differed from Boughton in that they possessed alumni as well as faculty status. Wallace had actually preceded Champion as acting pastor of the First Baptist Church, where he inspired the congregation to new levels of interest and engagement. In attacking two such stalwarts in the college community, Champion skated on thin ice.

Champion also alleged that several of his predecessors had been driven away from McMinnville by the same liberal influences that worked against him: "Having disposed of one pastor, the sport of killing becomes a fixed habit." This charge led Deacon A.C. Chandler, a McMinnville College trustee and son of its first president, to poll five of Champion's predecessors. Each expressed confidence in the McMinnville faculty, denying all reports of dissension.

Not surprisingly, given the historically warm relations between the church and the college that gave it birth, the First Baptist deacons, trustees, and finance committee scheduled a vote of no confidence in Champion for June 7, 1917. Results of a straw poll unanimous in favor of his ouster went to Champion by telegram on May 27, giving him the option of resigning. He seized the opportunity, and his campaign ended.

Champion's campaign did its damage, however, for Wallace followed Boughton in resigning from the college. He viewed his support from Riley and the trustees as equivocal, for though he retained his position, he was asked not to teach in the Bible department. In 1930, a year before Riley retired, Linfield made amends by awarding Wallace an honorary doctorate.

landlord by failing to pay their business taxes. On at least one occasion, college treasurer A.L. Veazie had to pay back taxes on a Spokane property to avoid its forfeiture.

Putting Frances Linfield's bequest into full perspective after all these years does not diminish its importance. The college ultimately realized $250,000 by slowly selling off the properties in the 1940s. More critically, Mrs. Linfield emulated her friend Leonard Riley in selflessly devoting her talents to the welfare of students for no remuneration beyond the annuity and management stipend. She lived simply and regularly contributed to scholarships and special projects at the college. An accomplished woman with a fine education, fluent in French and German, she served as a model to the community. Her wise judgment also helped to keep the college on an even keel. In coming forward at a critical juncture with the largest individual gift to the college to that time, Mrs. Linfield renewed much-needed institutional self-confidence.

For his part, Dr. Riley worked tirelessly to foster a Christian character within the students of the now-renamed Linfield College. His personality and stature with the trustees meant that he brooked no opposition, whether in suspending students for use of tobacco (even off campus), or in enforcing standards of Christian education in the classroom. He responded decisively, for example, to a letter from a local clergyman who questioned a textbook used in an ethics class. The president marched into the classroom of Frederick G. Boughton, registrar and professor of philosophy, to confiscate all nineteen copies of the text, including Boughton's. He later explained to the complainant: "I paid $1.50 to $2.00 apiece for each of these books, a sum I cannot afford to spend in that way, but I have done it gladly rather than have it go out that when I discovered anything like that I did not do all I possibly could to completely root out the offense." Riley confessed that he had not yet read the book, but expressed confidence in his friend's characterization of it as a dangerous secularized introduction to ethics.

Riley likewise inveighed against the teaching of Darwin-

ian theory at the college. Not all faculty members concurred with this official view. They did not dare, however, defend the theory of evolution outright. Rather, they explained that they sought merely to prepare Christian men and women for views likely to be encountered in the larger world. Students should, they held, be inoculated against error by learning of such theories in the Christian confines of Pioneer Hall. To his credit, Riley defended faculty members who took this route, but only after they had submitted to a thorough examination, sometimes by him and sometimes by the trustee-led board of visitors.

In such matters "Old Mac" and Linfield reflected the inner struggles of many early-twentieth-century church-related colleges in the escalating debate between modernity and traditionalism. Modernists favored jazz music, flouted prohibition, and at least entertained materialistic accounts of nature. Traditionalists condemned jazz, railed against "demon rum," and upheld biblical accounts of human origins and destiny. The famous Scopes Trial of 1925 sensationally dramatized this modernist-traditionalist rift. Few church-related colleges sided with the modernists, for they answered to constituencies generally outraged by the "dangerous" new ideas creeping into education. President Riley, attuned to his fellow clergymen's hostility to any deviation from approved "New Testament teaching," nonetheless heeded faculty reminders that freedom of conscience also represented a central Baptist value. While personally committed to a fundamentalist understanding of religion and the Bible, he

Left: 1928, In a gesture typifying the city's love for "its" college, members of the McMinnville Chamber of Commerce give treasurer Charles Kopf (in glasses with hand on check) a contribution of $27,646.30.

1903, Wooden footbridge across Cozine Creek served as the Lover's Lane until its demise in the 1960s.

granted others a surprising degree of intellectual latitude, especially given his conservative personal beliefs (see "Champion's Campaign," p. 56).

With crucial bolstering from Emanuel Northup and Frances Ross Linfield, President Riley constructed a genuine college out of the glimmerings foreshadowed decades earlier by the ambitious curriculum of President Bailey and the sturdy labors of President Brownson. The proof lies in the achievements of graduates of this era. Member of the class of 1910, Olof Larsell (see "Trustee and Teacher," p. 106) later became a prominent board chairman, instructor at the University of Oregon School of Medicine, and Fulbright Scholar to Sweden. Caroll H. Woody in 1911 and H. Reginald Bowler in 1912 each received Rhodes Scholarships. Their classmate, George Stewart, Jr., won the state oratorical contest, having graciously stepped aside from the Rhodes competition to let Bowler compete in his final year of eligibility. Such successes, plus the improved physical plant and financial support that made them possible, led the college to unconditional recognition by the U.S. Bureau of Education in 1922 and accreditation by the Northwest Association of Secondary and Higher Schools in 1925.

Frances Linfield resigned as dean of women in 1928 and the next year Emanuel Northup retired after forty-one years of teaching. President Riley followed these two into retirement in 1931, concluding twenty-five years of strenuous service that included salvaging a college on the verge of collapse, building a $1,000,000 endowment, constructing Melrose Hall (see "Treat's Treat," p. 55), and skillfully negotiating between fundamentalist impulse and academic freedom. In 1929, student Philip Renshaw began a lifelong affiliation with the college that led him to become its second-longest-serving trustee (1957 to 2003). Renshaw had selected Linfield as a place whose Christian precepts might preserve him from the temptations encountered during a year-and-a-half tour of the eastern United States. But as he regularly joked, "After six weeks under Leonard Riley, I realized I had overcorrected." Still, as a direct consequence of his Linfield experience, Renshaw tirelessly championed and supported the enduring value of his liberal education and the alma mater that had made it possible. Renshaw thus embodied the complex legacy of Leonard Riley, stiff-necked in enforcing what today appear narrow canons of personal morality, yet visionary enough to mold a substantial college with enough promise to attract a modernist successor, Dr. Elam Anderson. ∎

Opposite: *1925-26 faculty.* Front row, left to right: *William Reinhard Frerichs, Greek and German; Maurice Earle Pettit, physical education director and coach; Emanuel Northup, mathematics and dean of faculty; Kenneth Scott Latourette, alumnus and guest; Leonard W. Riley, president; Frances Eleanor Ross Linfield, practical ethics and dean of women; Charles Kopf, treasurer; Alice Clement, piano and organ and dean of the conservatory; Gustav Reinhold Schlauch, history.* Second row, left to right: *William Charles Gregory, physics; Lebbeus Smith Shumaker, philosophy and dean of men; William James Sly, religious education; John Kenneth Riley, registrar and librarian; Margaret Leota Mann, stenography and typewriting; Margaret Ramsey, mathematics; James Arthur Macnab, biology and geology; Adelaide Walker, French.* Back rows, left to right: *George Woodford Payne, Latin; William Jabez Jerome, political and social sciences; Herschel Edgar Hewitt, physics; Eugene Stark Gardiner, English; Arne Sigurd Jensen, education; unidentified; Marion E. Bollen, public speaking; Anna Lavina Beebe, voice.*

Linfield College Faculty, 1925-1926

The Untold Story

The foundation laid by President Riley proved stable enough to support Linfield's relative prosperity even as the Great Depression unfolded. Because the trustees and president maintained a conservative investment strategy, the college survived the worst of the stock market crash of 1929. It helped that, thanks to Frances Linfield, nearly a third of the endowment lay in property, which did not suffer the losses incurred in stocks. During the 1930s the endowment remained intact, an across-the-

President Elam Anderson and President Emeritus Leonard Riley, circa 1932-37

Opposite: *1938, International Week.* Left to right: *Joe Medicine Crow, Julia Blanchard, Esther Brick, Paul Louie, Margaret Ryan, Charles Manning*

board cut in salaries proved temporary, and healthy enrollment continued. Acknowledging a shortage of cash among students and their families, college officials readily accepted contributions of meat, grains, and produce.

One should not, of course, mistake relative prosperity for abundance. A 1928 comparison of salaries among similar institutions nationwide rated Linfield's average of $2,250 annually for full professors to be poor, earning a rating of one on a five-point scale. This fact reflected a college culture common in religiously affiliated schools, where teaching was regarded as a vocation presuming some degree of personal financial sacrifice. At the same time, the college used its resources effectively on behalf of students. Linfield rated four (good) on a student-to-faculty ratio of eleven to one. In annual operating expense per student, the college rated two (fair) at $256.

When Riley retired in 1931, the trustees found themselves in the unprecedented position of pursuing a number of qualified candidates to succeed him. While conducting their deliberations, they asked William J. Frerichs, dean of

faculty and professor of German, to serve during the academic year 1931-32 as acting president.

A Modernist President

These efforts led to the selection of Dr. Elam J. Anderson, a man well suited to move the college into a new era. Matching Riley in energy and devotion to Christian education, Anderson also held a progressive and expansive outlook in areas where Riley had proven conservative and restrained. A graduate of Drake University, Anderson began graduate study and taught for three years at Cornell University before he completed a doctorate in education at the University of Chicago. This made him the college's first president to earn a PhD in an academic subject rather than hold a master of theology or doctor of divinity degree. Before reaching Linfield, Anderson had spent fourteen years in China. Initially a professor of music and education at the University of Shanghai, he later directed schools in East China for the American Baptist Foreign Mission Society and eventually became superintendent of the Shanghai American School. Anderson

Dr. Elam J. Anderson, president, 1932 to 1938

Opposite: *1937, Debate team departing for Bakersfield, California, for forensics tournament.* Left to right: *Mark Nickerson, Aline Boswell, Josephine Cornacchia, Minna Rattey (coach/chaperone), Wilhemina Walpert, Bob Boyd*

Conversant with educational trends nationally and internationally, Anderson devised a New Linfield Plan for the curriculum in 1933. It inaugurated what has since become a familiar emphasis on "general education" in the first two years of matriculation. Under the New Linfield Plan, initial common courses prescribed for every student aimed to produce "educated citizens." Students then followed individualized interests on the way toward becoming "useful citizens." Predictably, given his extensive experience in China, Anderson's plan included a rich international emphasis stressing the study of contemporary civilizations, world literature, and foreign languages. Anderson also recruited a number of Asian students to Linfield College.

Anderson tirelessly promoted the college, accepting more than 200 speaking engagements a year. He bolstered community relations by pioneering the college's initial foray into adult education, charging tuition of only one dollar per course for noncommercial subjects. He maintained ties with local and national Baptist organizations, as had Riley, but his reach extended into national educational and scholarly organizations as well. It is no accident that in 1936, at the height of Anderson's presidency, Linfield appeared on the "approved list" of the American Association of Universities.

In the final analysis, Anderson's greatest legacy lay in developing a robust spirit of partnership among the administration, faculty, and students. Off-campus prohibitions on the use of tobacco and on dancing ended, though the bans remained on campus (see "Shall We Dance at Linfield?" p. 77). Student responsiveness to gatherings at the president's house (located in what has become Potter Hall) had been respectful under Riley but became notably genial and enthusiastic under Anderson. His letters to clergy and other objectors to alleged non-Christian teaching at the college provide a study in artful mediation as he defused critical animus while defending the faculty's prerogative to seek and speak truth. Anderson followed Riley in citing the "inoculation" defense—because students would invariably confront challenging modern ideas in the world beyond

authored two books, one on the efficiency of English language instruction in China, the other an appreciation of Western classical music written for a Chinese audience. His liberal theological bent inclined him toward inclusive cultural perspectives.

Arriving in 1932, Anderson wasted no time putting his imprint on Linfield College. Deeming housing deficient, especially for women, he used general college revenues to erect Isabel Grover Cottage (now Grover Hall) in 1934. Jane C. Failing Hall (named for the wife of trustee and major donor James Failing) followed in 1935, and a men's dormitory (later Mac Hall) in 1937. His most important contribution to the academic infrastructure of the college lay in the opening of the new Northup Library in 1936 (see "The Library: Nook to Nicholson," p. 125).

McMINNVILLE
COLUMBIA MARKET
Tasty SALAD QT. DRESSING 15¢
TUNA FLAKES 10¢
TRY SUNKIST • SPECIAL PRICES
RANGES NOW

Linfield, they should first encounter them as part of an education equipping them for intelligent critique. Anderson's passion for engaging ideas differentiated him markedly from Riley's more grudging posture.

Athletics reached new heights, mainly due to Henry W. Lever, professor of physical education, appointed by Riley in 1930. Lever coached all men's sports and proved especially effective in basketball, where over fifteen seasons he compiled a 173-109 record. President Anderson quickly came to terms with the importance of athletics as a means of bolstering support for the college among local businessmen and as a venue for satisfying the cocurricular interests of students. Multiple tennis courts appeared on campus during his presidency, as did a field house and a significantly improved football field.

Anderson's tenure, in fact, included several notable events in the history of Linfield football. In 1934, he suspended all participation in athletics with Willamette University until a Willamette student confessed to painting a "WU" on the pillars of Melrose Hall and sawing off Linfield's goalposts following his school's victory. It took over a year of negotiation before Willamette and Linfield agreed to compete again. Perhaps because Linfield did not play Willamette in the ensuing year, the Lever-coached football team claimed its first conference championship, the sole such title until 1956. The program for the winning game, 14-0, over the College of Idaho mentions two important Lever protégés. Roy Helser, later Linfield's baseball coach, missed the game at running back due to a broken ankle; Paul Durham, destined as football coach in 1949 to defeat Willamette for the first time in twenty-five years, earned commendation as "A candidate for all-star honors in his fourth season on the Baptist line."

Just as football fortunes could swing unpredictably, Anderson's ability to foster harmony among Baptist supporters of the college began to wane after his earlier successes. His perceived laxity toward student conduct provoked uneasiness about the Christian commitment of the college. The global emphasis and national prominence of the

New Linfield Plan created the fear that local voices went unheeded at the college. The Oregon State Baptist Convention thus put Linfield College under its microscope in 1936 and 1937. Whereas the earlier uneasiness of 1917 had focused on select faculty members, clearly exempting President Riley, the revived concern extended more generally. Though the Convention was too polite to say so directly, its reservations targeted presidential leadership. Anderson's less authoritarian style suggested a loss of commitment to the traditional formula of *Christo et Veritas*, wherein Christ came first and truth second.

In the end Anderson's openness and diplomacy won the day when a supportive faculty answered doubters by unanimously endorsing a statement of Christian faith. Yet in 1938, the trustees once again investigated charges against Linfield faculty and students, this time for political radicalism, not doctrinal error. Professor Harold Elkinton, head of Linfield's business program, provoked scrutiny by challenging an anti-Soviet speaker at a meeting of the local Kiwanis club. Word of Elkinton's supposed communist sympathies spread, surfacing even in the *Oregonian*. At Anderson's request, Elkinton wrote an "apology" that defended intellectual questioning as essential to honest inquiry.

A second dramatic incident arose in May 1938, when a visiting campus evangelist alleged that "fourteen communist students" had petitioned to boycott his preaching, both on campus and at McMinnville's First Baptist Church. The Salem *Statesman* reported the boycott as more evidence of radical teaching at Linfield. After interviewing the students, Anderson issued a rejoinder that they had merely objected to the speaker's "emotional evangelism" rather than to the content of his preaching. He pointedly rejected labeling the students as communists.

In response to these incidents, the trustees created the first of two notorious investigatory committees, this one a Special Committee on Radicalism. No explicit record exists to explain the role these travails played in President Anderson's 1938 decision to become president of the University of

1935-36, Henry W. Lever

Opposite: *1941, Driver Homer Groening escorts his future wife, May Queen Margaret Wiggum, during the annual May Day parade in downtown McMinnville (see "For Trivia Buffs," p. 93).*

Connecting Learning
The Conservatory

McMinnville College instituted a Conservatory of Music at the turn of the twentieth century. The label reflected hopeful thinking more than sober reality, but the name was so popular with music faculty and students that they held onto it for nearly half a century.

Aspirations for a music curriculum surfaced as early as 1872, when the first college catalog announced a position for "Teacher of Music" still to be filled. Compared to the maximum $10.50 per term charged for the Classical Department (responsible for traditional collegiate study), the fees needed to support the music instructor were steep: $15 for a twelve-week term for "instrumental instruction," plus $3 a term for "use of the piano or organ." Nevertheless, in 1890 the number of students paying tuition for music (84) exceeded those enrolled in the collegiate department (81).

The first music teacher of record, Miss Laura A. Gotra, appears on the books in 1882. Healthy revenues in 1899 emboldened the trustees to hire the first "Principal" of the Conservatory of Music: Miss R. M. Trumbull, "a brilliant pianist, a teacher of marked ability, both in Instrumental and Vocal; a lecturer of recognized talent, and also a musical composer of more than ordinary merit." Miss Trumbull borrowed from the poet Goethe the conservatory's motto, "Ohne Hast, Ohne Rast" (Without Hurry, Without Rest).

Not coincidentally, the relatively lucrative conservatory played a significant role in President Leonard Riley's efforts to save the college during his tenure. Under the leadership of Carrie Casler Potter, who assumed her post in 1904, the program generated sufficient revenues to support the construction of Music Hall in 1908.

When Elam Anderson became president in 1932, however, the conservatory's focus on producing professional musicians gave way to an emphasis on music as one of the liberal arts. The college catalog indicates that music became a department in a newly created Division of Fine Arts during Anderson's first year in office. Mention of a conservatory did not entirely disappear from college publications for a number of years, as the terms "department" and "conservatory" both surface in published materials. But while the much-loved Alice Clement continued for a time to be identified as "Dean of the Conservatory of Music," by 1944 she became simply "Professor of Music"—a sign that the conservatory had finally receded into history.

1909, Music Hall (later Colonial Hall) and Pioneer Hall

1906, McMinnville College glee club and band

Redlands. In some quarters, his defenses of Elkinton and the protesting students doubtless vindicated the earlier suspicions of the State Baptist Convention. Judging his usefulness to have reached its high-water mark, Anderson may have sought to remove himself as a target for future attacks on the college. He remained well regarded at Linfield and returned to warm welcomes on numerous occasions. After his death in 1944, his widow, Colena, joined the Linfield faculty, serving two terms as dean of women, and receiving the title professor emerita from the board in 1964 (see "Three Exemplary Deans," p. 114).

Clouds of Dissension and War

The trustees tapped one of their own to become the college's next president: Rev. William G. Everson, pastor of the First Baptist Church of Portland. While the choice of Everson seemed ideal to heal rifts between the college and the state's Baptists, Linfield would again become a target of suspicion under his watch, at least as much due to dissension within the Baptist Convention itself as to events at the college. It did not help that in Everson's first year the specter of college radicalism surfaced when Professor Roy D. Mahaffey directed in Portland the student-authored *Judge Not,* a play raising questions about the U.S. death penalty.

Everson possessed a novel background for a college president and pastor. As a colonel in the U.S. Army, he had commanded the American sector in Italy during World War I. He later rose to the rank of major general and served as National Guard chief from 1929 to 1931. With the darkening war clouds of the late 1930s, his military background benefited the college. A generous and open man, Everson held more conservative beliefs than Anderson, but not so conservative as those expected of him by the fundamentalist faction of the Oregon State Baptist Convention. He eventually vacated office rather than take sides in simmering local, regional, and national controversies over fidelity to Baptist principles. Everson left it for his successor, Harry Dillin, to affiliate nationally with the more liberal emergent American Baptist Convention.

In other respects Everson found himself as much a captive of his times as President Boardman had been fifty years earlier. In this case, war rather than national financial collapse circumscribed Everson's options. During his tenure the college constructed only one building, the present colonial-style president's house. Meanwhile, enrollment melted away as college-age males enlisted in droves in the armed forces. Fifteen Linfield National Guard members were activated in 1940. Following the December 1941 attack on Pearl Harbor, the college modified its curriculum to accommodate some degree of military training, though it never received the Reserve Officer Training Corps status that Everson sought. By 1943 student enrollment dwindled to 225, 80 percent of them women. Both faculty and trustees, including board chairman Dr. Winifred H. Bueerman, also left the college to defend their country.

Despite the national emergency, the factions within the Oregon State Baptist Convention remained contentious. Unconvinced by the 1938 declaration of Christian faith endorsed by Linfield's faculty, the Convention passed two new resolutions on April 9, 1942. The first alleged that the college harbored "certain reported teachings and statements in certain lectures, that are seemingly definitely opposed to the Christian concept and purpose of its founding." The second resolution charged the president with oversight: "Be it resolved that we voice our pleasure in the expressed ideals of Dr. William G. Everson for the Christian standards of the school, and that we give to him hearty support in the carrying out of these ideals."

Before perspective could be gained and a plan undertaken for dealing with thirteen "evidential letters" supporting the allegations in the first resolution, Everson surprised both the Linfield board and the Convention by resigning in February of 1943. A follow-up resolution passed by the Convention that same year regretted that Everson "found it necessary to resign" but expressed "delight in his resolute stand opposing the faculty's recommendation that dancing be permitted on the campus." This follow-up resolution indicates

Rose M. Trumbull, principal of the conservatory, 1886 to 1904

that social conservatism marched hand in hand with educational conservatism for a plurality of the Convention's delegates. As with Anderson's departure, no documentary evidence suggests the specific reasoning behind Everson's resignation, but the political outlines remain clear. Everson chose not to press forward with the full agenda of the conservatives who claimed to be his champions.

If Everson could not himself heal the rifts within the Oregon State Baptist Convention (as no single person could), his resignation attracted attention of a sort that Elam Anderson's had not. Chastened conservatives would discover over the long run that they had overreached, but in the short run, several Linfield faculty members suffered the brunt of their attack.

The man who inherited the combined threats of wartime low enrollment and an intrusive State Baptist Convention was Harry L. Dillin, a member of the faculty and a man already entrusted with many administrative responsibilities. With a bachelor's degree from St. Stephen's (now Bard) College and a master's degree from the University of North Carolina, Dillin did not complete his PhD either at North Carolina or the University of Michigan, where he continued his studies—a deficit that produced conflict later in his tenure. Hired by Leonard Riley to teach math and economics in 1931, Dillin became a favorite both of Elam Anderson and William Everson. In addition to faculty duties, Dillin served eleven years as treasurer for the Associated Students of Linfield College. When external investment advisors counseled the trustees during the Depression to sell off the college's diminished stock portfolio to invest in government bonds, Dillin strongly protested. President Anderson then made him the official watchdog of Linfield's portfolio. Ultimately, Dillin proved correct: selling would have missed the upturn in the stock market. Shortly after Dillin's ascension to the Linfield presidency, the University of Redlands, under Elam Anderson's leadership, granted him an honorary doctoral degree.

Left: *June 7, 1945, Launch of USS* Linfield Victory

Connecting Life
Linfield at War

Though McMinnville College was founded prior to the American Civil War, its place on the frontier insulated it from that terrible conflict. No records have come to light of any founders or students serving for either the Union or the Confederacy. Oregon Baptists did split between pro- and antislavery factions, with McMinnville College subscribing to the antislavery cause.

The first recorded alumni to die during combat—Bertie Clark and Frank Hibbs—participated with at least seventeen other McMinnville College students in the Spanish-American War of 1898. In addition, eleven nurses and two interns left the Good Samaritan Hospital to provide medical services in that conflict.

World War I found McMinnville College graduate (class of 1901) and army Lieutenant Leonard Hopfield drilling roughly seventy-five men from his alma mater for enlistment at the end of the spring semester of 1917. Approximately 167 McMinnville College men became veterans of the conflict, with at least 6 killed in the line of duty. Good Samaritan sent off 103 graduate nurses to army hospitals, many serving in France.

Linfield's mobilization for World War II matched the size and gravity of that conflict. Over 500 alumni, faculty members, and trustees saw service, with 25 named as dead or missing in action. Nurses from Good Samaritan also rallied to the cause, with over 100 enlisting. In 1945 a liberty ship, the USS *Linfield Victory*, was commissioned at the Oregon Shipbuilding Corporation in Portland.

Aviator and navy Lieutenant Randy Scoggan went missing in action during the Korean War. Films of that war's soldiers being treated for battlefield wounds were shown during a 1952 chapel program to bolster Linfield's turnout for the annual Red Cross blood drive.

College draft deferments continued during the Vietnam War era but gave way to a draft lottery among all selective service registrants in December 1969. In a country deeply divided on the merits of the war, the student rights movement came to the fore at Linfield as across the country. According to *Linfield College Bulletin* records, which may not be exhaustive, at least six alumni died in Vietnam, including army Captain Richard Goss '54, army Lieutenant Ralph Leroy Williams '62, navy Lieutenant Stephen Richardson '63, navy Lieutenant Wayne Alan Armstrong '63, and Private First Class Michael Barrow '68. Army Lieutenant Paul H. Eklund '63 posthumously received Bronze Star and Silver Star medals.

The most recent Linfield graduate (class of 2000) to die in defense of country—army First Lieutenant Erik McCrae—died in Baghdad, Iraq, on June 4, 2004. Professor of English Lex Runciman published a tribute to McCrae in the fall 2004 edition of *The Linfield Magazine*.

Late 1960s, Susanne Morgenroth Eklund, class of 1963, widow of Paul Eklund, class of 1963, receives his Bronze and Silver Star medals. Others, left to right: *Mrs. Paul G. Eklund, mother of the deceased; Roger Eklund, class of 1968, brother; and Major General C.F. Leonard Jr.*

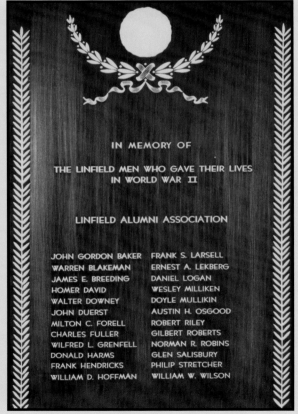

IN MEMORY OF
THE LINFIELD MEN WHO GAVE THEIR LIVES
IN WORLD WAR II

LINFIELD ALUMNI ASSOCIATION

JOHN GORDON BAKER	FRANK S. LARSELL
WARREN BLAKEMAN	ERNEST A. LEKBERG
JAMES E. BREEDING	DANIEL LOGAN
HOMER DAVID	WESLEY MILLIKEN
WALTER DOWNEY	DOYLE MULLIKIN
JOHN DUERST	AUSTIN H. OSGOOD
MILTON C. FORELL	ROBERT RILEY
CHARLES FULLER	GILBERT ROBERTS
WILFRED L. GRENFELL	NORMAN R. ROBINS
DONALD HARMS	GLEN SALISBURY
FRANK HENDRICKS	PHILIP STRETCHER
WILLIAM D. HOFFMAN	WILLIAM W. WILSON

World War II memorial plaque. The name of Hubert A. Santo was added subsequently.

1945, Student Body President Norman Goss. President Dillin, and Lieutenant A.L. Morris during presentation of flag from the USS Linfield Victory

From the start Dillin had to contend with the furor created by the State Baptist Convention resolutions. Over the summer of 1943, the trustees constituted a Special Committee on Religious Education and Investigation. The committee reviewed the ten accusatory letters from former Linfield students and three from clergymen, one a Presbyterian and the others Baptists. Next they interviewed, in person and in the presence of Dillin, four of the six professors against whom complaints were lodged. The other two, away from McMinnville for the summer, were invited to submit written responses to the allegations. Though not quite ready to endorse the evidence of un-Christian teachings at the college, the committee sent a somber message to the trustee Executive Committee:

> While we ought not and cannot reach conclusions even tentatively at present, we feel that we should report that some of the charges made are of a very serious nature and if substantiated should call for drastic action on the part of the Board. One student states that certain doctrines he believed in were ridiculed by a member of the Faculty. Another student is reported to have said, "When I came here, I knew what I believed in the Christian faith. I was considered a fundamentalist. Now I don't know what to believe. My mind is upset and I am graduating this June. My family say that I have become a modernist in faith." No more serious charge could be brought against a Christian College than to have students feel that the Christian teachings they have received from parents, Sunday School teachers or pastors are worthy of ridicule, or to have students graduate feeling that they have no positive Christian faith.

In this way the fundamentalist-modernist schism wracking the Oregon State Baptist Convention produced its own fissures at Linfield. Rather than continue unsuccessfully to dislodge modernist pastors (protected as they were by the Baptist practice of autonomy for local churches), the conservatives found a charge of "corrupting the youth" to be tailor-made for their doctrinal purge, since the college was not an autonomous congregation. What is more, their own convention held seats on the board of trustees, and they could press the special committee through their representative, W.A. Shanks.

These circumstances led Dillin to publish in the September-October 1943 *Oregon Baptist* a piece entitled "Greetings to our Baptist Friends," which concluded: "As President, may I . . . assure you that the college is as purposeful as were our founders and that our influence shall spread ever wider in the field of Christian education." Such efforts at appeasement failed to suffice, and in 1945 several faculty members resigned. At least one had been accused in the denunciatory letters received from ministers and students, allowing Dillin to demonstrate responsiveness to the Convention's resolutions. He simultaneously attained votes of confidence from the Washington State Baptist Convention and the North Idaho Baptist Convention. Because these two groups also held the right to nominate trustees, their support became crucial.

Dillin's failure to protect faculty members, as Riley had done in 1917 and Anderson in 1938, remains unaccountable. Perhaps as the first nonclergyman named to Linfield's presidency, he felt he had to exercise special rigor in enforcing standards of Christian belief. Indeed, he explicitly made "Christian character" a condition of employment at the college soon after these events. When he announced the departure of four additional faculty members in 1946, he told the trustees: "Most of the resignations from our staff were effected by your president that there might be a better-trained faculty, more co-operative and better fitted to the needs of a Christian educational institution such as this."

One resignation came from Dr. James A. Macnab, a professor of biology, and perhaps the most nationally prominent educator ever to teach at the college (see "'Prof.' and His Heirs," p. 71). Save for his unfortunate clash with Dillin, his many distinctions would likely have led to the naming of a building in his honor. For twenty-four years Macnab taught and conducted extended ecological research on Saddleback Mountain, inspiring two generations of biology majors to pursue advanced degrees. Students did not take kindly to news of Macnab's resignation. Five of them appeared before the Executive Committee when it considered the matter, urging its members to keep Macnab on the faculty. The committee members listened politely, dismissed the students, and then voted to endorse Dillin for having solicited the resignation.

It remains inconclusive that Macnab numbered among the original six faculty members interviewed by the religious investigations committee, though his teaching of evolution might well have caused his inclusion in that group. But Dillin's quest for a faculty "better suited to the needs of a Christian institution" clearly enabled him to rid the college of someone he regarded as a nuisance. Macnab had actively promoted the fledgling cause of the American Association of University Professors at Linfield, serving as its president at the time of his departure. Evidence also suggests that he made known his disapproval of Dillin for allegedly claiming to hold an earned PhD when in fact he did not.

This sad episode produced an equally sad coda. The charge that Dillin claimed against the facts to hold an earned PhD was revived in 1950 by several of Macnab's former students. They wrote the trustees a letter demanding that Dillin be sanctioned. The trustees investigated, vindicated Dillin, and wrote the group's leader a letter essentially warning that he and his associates were not to repeat such libelous charges on pain of prosecution by the college. The same charge against Dillin resurfaced in 1952 in a letter to the trustees from a retiring faculty member who was subsequently denied emeritus status by the board.

By the time of Macnab's resignation in 1946, the college stood on the verge of the most dramatic transformation in its history. Millions of soldiers returning from war in Europe, North Africa, and the Pacific took advantage of the Servicemen's Readjustment Act of 1944 (the G.I. Bill). In the nation at large, 2.6 million World War II veterans ultimately relied on the G.I. Bill for tuition and living stipends. Just over a thousand of them chose to apply their benefit to Linfield College.

Enrollment mushroomed from a wartime low of 225 in

Dr. James A. Macnab   *Dr. John Boling and student*   *Dr. Jane Claire Dirks-Edmunds*

Connecting Learning
"Prof" and His Heirs

Dr. James A. Macnab's students called him "Prof" out of respect for his demanding standards and the pride they took in meeting them, since nothing but their best work would satisfy him. Generations of high-achieving students looked back on his guidance as the formative experience of their intellectual lives.

The son of a Presbyterian minister, Macnab grew up in Roseburg, Oregon, and graduated from Albany College. After earning an MS in biology at the University of Nebraska, he arrived at Linfield in 1924. Together with Luther Taylor, professor of chemistry, and Herschel Hewitt, professor of physics, Macnab created a science curriculum as rich in ideas as the college remained poor in laboratory resources. The pragmatic spirit of Linfield science took shape through the example of these three faculty giants.

Macnab unquestionably spearheaded science education at Linfield, as attested in *The Origins of American Scientists* (1952). The book ranks Linfield among the top 10 percent of liberal arts colleges nationwide in the per-capita production of graduates earning doctoral degrees in science. Its authors note:

> The biology department of Linfield is one of the most interesting science departments reviewed in this study. Its brilliant achievement from 1928 to 1939 appears to be attributable almost solely to the unusual talent of its one faculty member and chairman, J.A. Macnab. . . .

An attempt of some sort should be made to explain Macnab's success. One important factor was his devotion to research, in which his students participated regularly. In preparation for his doctoral thesis, Macnab undertook an ecology study of a tract of Douglas fir in the region. This enterprise continued for more than a decade and provided a constant opportunity for his students to participate in his researches. A second contributing feature was probably the fact that Macnab had very high academic standards.

His ecological survey of Saddleback Mountain, near McMinnville, became the basis for his own PhD, awarded from the University of Nebraska in 1944, twenty years after he arrived at Linfield. Among the eighteen PhD graduates whose accomplishments earned Linfield its stellar ranking in the national study, sixteen had been mentored by Macnab. In 1946, however, President Harry Dillin forced Macnab's resignation.

Fortunately, Macnab's positive influence at Linfield persisted in the persons of two Linfield graduates who went on to earn biology PhDs before returning to teach at the college. John Boling assumed the department chairmanship on Macnab's departure and, while of a gentler nature, earned equal affection among his students. Jane Claire Dirks-Edmunds continued the research on Saddleback Mountain begun by Prof and, along with Boling, inspired many more Linfield graduates to pursue careers in research or medicine. Following her retirement, Dirks-Edmunds published *Not Just Trees* (1999), a compelling account of the longitudinal forest study begun under Macnab and continued for sixty years by generation after generation of Linfield students.

1943-44 to 800 in 1946-47. Faculty ranks expanded as those who had gone off to war returned, among them Dr. Steine Jonasson in history, a recent flying instructor in Florida; Dr. "Hod" Terrell from English, a volunteer in the American Red Cross; Milo Wold from music, a veteran of the U.S. Army; and mathematician Margaret Ramsay, an instructor in officer training schools. In fall 1946, the college also added seventeen new faculty members, including alumnus Dr. Walter P. Dyke. The next year nine new faculty members were hired, and in 1948 eleven more joined the community, including Dr. Winthrop Dolan as professor of mathematics and dean of faculty, Dr. Gordon Frazee as assistant professor of religion, and Paul Durham as head football coach and assistant professor of physical education. A key generation had arrived.

Buildings and Baby Shows

Life changed at Linfield College with the G.I.s' arrival. The conservatives who had so praised Everson for rejecting the faculty's petition to allow dancing on campus did not stand a chance in the postwar era. President Dillin had raised this "social question" in his first report to the board, imploring the trustees to support the faculty position, as Anderson had done in 1936. For years the trustees had swept aside presidential eloquence on the issue but they could not resist the adamancy of mature, returning soldiers who literally voted with their feet. The ban on campus dancing officially fell in 1946, though the trustees stipulated that they were merely permitting, not approving, the practice. In 1947 they consoled themselves with the view that lifting the ban had actually resulted in less dancing than before among Linfield students. Because dancing could now occur on campus, they reasoned,

Left: 1945, President Dillin at start of construction on Cook Infirmary

Opposite: 1947, President Dillin crowns "Big Queen" Bernadette Hagedorn. Also pictured, left to right: Mrs. Maurice L. Cohn, daughter Sandy Cohn, Mrs. James Bennett, son Dan Bennett, and James Page (class of 1966). "The University Dames" (the Linfield wives' club) sponsored the baby shows until the early 1950s.

serious-minded students would continue as before, whereas the more rebellious need no longer make a show of their rebellion. *The Linfield Review* for those years shows that this conclusion contained more than a kernel of wishful thinking.

The postwar influx of new students posed a variety of other challenges for the college, including those of housing and educating them satisfactorily. Many students were married and starting families, as evidenced in national publicity Linfield received for its "Baby Shows." To house them, the college moved temporary married student student quarters

from decomissioned army bases but needed more. An astute manager, President Dillin recognized that such expansion would require the college to incur debt. Since Riley's days, the trustees had insisted that building funds be subscribed in advance. However, in deference to Dillin's financial expertise, they agreed to build on the promise of future revenues. Dillin argued that future rental income from residence halls as well as future increased tuition dollars from needed instructional facilities would cover costs in a fraction of the buildings' useful lives. Thus began President Dillin's "building

Left: *1952, Aerial view of campus from the east*

Opposite: *1950s, Students leaving Melrose Hall*

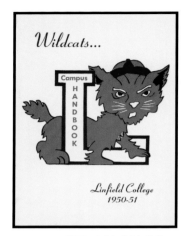

1950-51 Linfield College Campus Handbook

Right: 1956, Bill Anderson working as a disc jockey at the radio station

fund," a method of internal accounting that satisfied the local banks' desire for collateral but kept endowment earnings fungible for any uses the trustees deemed appropriate. As federal monies became available to private colleges, the building fund expanded to include bonding from this source.

This building fund did not operate as the exercise in promiscuous financing that a Leonard Riley might have claimed. Riley, after all, had restored confidence in the college by using endowment earnings to eradicate accumulated debt, and he was not about to incur new debt. Initially, Dillin committed the college to borrowing only small amounts to meet immediate needs. Opening the first new instructional space,

as with married student housing, rested upon the acquisition of donated surplus buildings from various military bases.

Dillin strove by various measures to keep the price of new construction as low as possible. In 1945, to relieve a shortage of nails locally, Dillin and his wife collected enough gas rationing cards to drive across the country to a national church meeting. They stopped in many small towns along the way to purchase kegs of nails, shipping them back to McMinnville. Later, Dillin served as the college's general contractor, employing local builder Dwight Miller as day-to-day foreman. Toward the middle of his presidency, in fact, Dillin found himself targeted by labor unions when his

Connecting Life
Shall We Dance at Linfield?

In spring of 1936, ten students met with President Elam Anderson for a "frank discussion of the dancing problem as it concerns Linfield College." The students later proposed that a summary of their discussion be printed as an editorial in the school newspaper. Anderson, who had ended the prohibition on dancing off campus, would not allow the debate to be published, but did send the material to the trustees for discussion. The arguments against dancing prevailed with the trustees, and continued to do so until 1946.

The Arguments Against:

Dancing involves sex stimulation—a stimulation that often leads to prostitution.

The type of music used in the dance, according to a noted musician, is "immoral" because it stimulates the body in a way that stirs sex desire. Also, dance music depraves the appreciation for finer music.

It creates restlessness and morbid thinking with regard to sex.

It conduces to self-abandonment, which is destructive of poise and self-control.

The stuffiness of the dance hall and of perspiration is not sanitary.

Drinking is often associated with dancing.

Conducting a dance is a lazy way to entertain. Young people need to learn originality in entertainment, and if Linfield College organizations were permitted to conduct dances, they would over-do the dance and lose an important part of education—namely, learning to have fun that requires intelligence.

Dancing is undesirable at Linfield because many parents have sent young people to Linfield with the understanding that the college does not sponsor dancing. In case of a dance, the non-dancers would feel neglected because unable to participate. Also, many of the donors gave their endowments with the stipulation, at least implied if not expressed, that dancing not be permitted at Linfield. We must not break faith with those who have put their faith in the college.

1949, Couples dancing at the annual Intercollegiate Knights Sweetheart Ball

It is not the place of a sincere Christian to dance; he has too many other more important things to do.

Would you be willing to take Christ to a dance?

The Arguments For:

The sex stimulation of the dance is not intense or harmful; as a matter of fact, a certain degree of it is desirable for wholesome sex development.

All dance music is not sensual to the point of immorality. Some dance music is really lovely and worthy of appreciation.

Dancing provides release of sex tensions and of restlessness; there is nothing better than exercise—and dancing is good exercise—for working off these natural tensions. It develops gracefulness and imparts poise and confidence for social participation, especially in mixed groups. It helps men and women learn to associate wholesomely with one another.

Dancing, as it could be conducted at Linfield, would necessarily be under healthful conditions.

Drinking is not necessarily associated with dancing, and at Linfield College students would learn to appreciate the desirability of dancing without drink.

Other means of entertainment may be well for small groups, but for large-scale entertainment, dancing is the simplest and the most convenient form of entertainment.

The disapproval of some parents should not deter those who wish to dance. The number of dances permitted could be restricted so that all students might find their opportunity for social activity.

The college is for education. People are bound to dance in any case; is it not better to provide college-conducted dances of a wholesome kind, so that students may learn to appreciate the better kind of conduct at a dance, rather than be free to attend public dances as at present? In this way Linfield may educate students to a higher type of dancing.

The sincere Christian must develop his social side of life. The dance can be wholesome. If it be un-Christian as at present conducted, is it not possible to make it Christian?

practice of using college employees and students on construction jobs drew charges that he violated the Davis-Bacon Act, which required that construction workers be paid locally prevailing wages on certain projects. On another occasion, federal housing officials delayed a request for bonding authority for Anderson Hall, questioning "a loan to an institution which builds its own buildings rather than by means of a contractor."

However novel his approach, Dillin oversaw the addition of more square footage to the campus than any other president. Residence halls constructed during his tenure (1943 to 1968) include Latourette, Memorial, Miller, Campbell, Anderson, Larsell, Hewitt, and Whitman. Both Failing and Grover received third floors. The acquisition of multiple nearby properties added an additional eighteen acres to the campus. Two buildings purchased as army surplus provided expanded classroom, teaching, research, and student areas and became the first Frerichs Hall (fine arts building) and Science Hall (now Taylor). These additions continued with the openings of Cook Infirmary, Cozine Hall, Riley Center, Graf Hall, Renshaw Hall, and a new cafeteria, appropriately named Dillin Hall (after both the president and his wife, Irene). Northup Library was expanded; Pioneer Hall was refurbished and reinforced with internal steel bracing. Dillin's considerable energies also benefited the athletic program, which inaugurated Memorial Stadium, a state-of-the-art cinder track encircling Maxwell Field, and a new baseball field. A new boiler plant provided the augmented steam heating necessary for the expanded infrastructure. Two fraternities, Delta Tau Delta and Alpha Tau Omega, secured college mortgages to construct houses, while others were allowed to purchase surplus college houses. Dillin also restored the practice, common before the Riley era, of granting mortgages to faculty members, including these properties in the real estate portion of the endowment. Last but not least, the Linfield Research Institute (LRI), begun under Dillin's watch, came to occupy Linke Hall, added as an affiliated property just south of campus.

Significant improvements to the compensation and support of professional employees also occurred under Dillin's leadership. Faculty and staff salaries grew, assisted by a major grant from the Ford Foundation in 1955. Benefits expanded to include tuition exchange at cooperating sister colleges (1955), a two-dollar-a-month-per-employee contribution toward health insurance (1958), and a retirement contribution of 5 percent, shared between the college and employee, on the first $4,800 of salary (1960). The curriculum embraced internships (1944), a nursing reciprocity agreement with the University of Oregon (1950), elementary education certification (1955), and majors in political science (1957), social science (1958), and art (1967). In 1955 the National Association of Schools of Music accredited Linfield's music program for the first time, and three years later the college launched a Junior Year Abroad opportunity. In 1957 physics major James P. Gunton became the third student in college history to win a Rhodes Scholarship. Modest summer sabbaticals for senior faculty and academic-year sabbaticals for junior faculty, begun in 1965, enabled further university study and advanced degree completion (rather than fostering ongoing faculty research and scholarship as occurs today).

Establishment of the Linfield Research Institute remains the most significant achievement of the Dillin era, though Dillin himself voiced ambivalence about it to board chairman Marshall Dana. The LRI story remains compelling because an undergraduate college with virtually no tradition of promoting research among its faculty seems unlikely soil for one of the first research institutes on the West Coast. Its centrality to the story of Linfield College received confirmation when, in 2001, the college more than doubled its physical size thanks to earlier events at LRI and the growth of business enterprises spun off from the institute. LRI sprang almost entirely from the determination of alumnus and faculty member Dr. Walter Dyke, the son of Walter Dyke senior, another alumnus and long-serving Linfield trustee (see "Dyke's Pragmatic Legacy," p. 123).

Opposite: *1950s, Dr. Walter Dyke and student*

1950, Left to right, Beryl Campbell, Tuffy Rheulan, and Lu Cranage study in their residence hall room.

The younger Dyke returned to the college in 1946 to head the physics department after having served as director of radar research at the Massachusetts Institute of Technology. A newly minted PhD from the University of Washington, the thirty-two-year-old Dyke earned an annual salary of $2,600 in contrast to a typical starting salary of $1,750. Within less than a year, he secured a $5,000 grant from Research Corporation and prompted adoption of a trustee policy statement encouraging research and permitting reduced teaching loads for those successful at it. Thus, by equating research with the systematic discovery of new knowledge as opposed to the effort to keep one's lectures current, Dyke challenged a Linfield tradition that had defined faculty achievement solely in terms of teaching excellence.

Dyke's scientific success reinforced his message. Dr. Kenneth Trolan, a Linfield classmate of Dyke's, soon joined the faculty as a teacher and assistant director of research in physics. Dr. Winthrop Dolan, dean of faculty and professor of mathematics, provided mathematical calculations for their efforts to refine a cathode ray tube developed in the basement of Melrose Hall. Tireless and exacting, Dyke worked sixteen-hour days and expected the same from his colleagues. By 1954, the team's investigations into potential industrial applications of their patented field emission cathode ray tube brought in $77,000 in grants and employed seventeen people. By 1955, the grant total had risen to $129,000.

Given such results, Dyke argued that scientific research at Linfield needed to have its own designated home. Despite President Dillin's reservations that a research institute did not fit the mission of a teaching college, the trustees appointed a special committee to recommend next steps. Working swiftly and following a model laid out by Dyke, the committee secured passage of eight resolutions brought to the trustees at a special meeting on October 22, 1955. The board authorized the filing of articles of incorporation for the Linfield Research Institute and named seven Linfield trustees, including Dillin, to the LRI board to serve alongside five at-large members. In exchange for annual rent of $20,000, the college agreed to provide space to LRI in Melrose and the vacated Colonial Hall. The Linfield Research Institute bought all patents developed by Dyke's team for $50,000, with the understanding that payment would not be due until LRI had begun earning revenues on licenses associated with the patents.

In a collection of essays entitled *Linfield's Hundred Years* (published to celebrate the college's 1956 centennial), Steine Jonasson offered several pages on LRI that anticipated a prosperous future. In fact, by 1957, LRI grants had grown to $500,000 and were managed by forty employees. But such success bred pressing challenges, not the least of which involved the continuing lack of space for expansion. With commercial application of the institute's patents at hand, a split between Linfield and LRI loomed. Jonasson, dean of administration, helped negotiate the separation in a less than amiable atmosphere, and Dyke took his field emissions research outside the college.

Both Linfield and Dyke had legitimate concerns. Though gratified by the accomplishments of the institute, the trustees worried that these rested too heavily on the indispensable role of a single person. Early on, the college had secured modest loans for the institute, but as the scope of projects grew, the sums requested for institute support expanded as well. The institute also needed new, purpose-built facilities at which Dillin and the trustees balked. A divorce seemed imminent when, in the words accompanying a special trustee ballot of June 10, 1958, an "almost providential" solution presented itself. McMinnville's Linke family agreed to provide thirty-six adjacent acres south of campus and to secure the mortgage on a new LRI building.

This resolution did not hold, however. With each man used to exercising full authority in his own sphere, tensions between Dillin and Dyke surfaced and collided with the robust economic prospects of LRI's technological break-throughs. Together these factors prompted Dyke to found Field Emission Corporation (Femcor) on the Linke property. On October 26, 1960, the Linfield trustees ratified a separation agreement whereby Femcor would not only repay the original $50,000 loan advanced by the college but also tender $10,000 a year, or 4 percent of profits to a maximum of $100,000, "in recognition of the risk taken by the College of its capital, name and reputation in sponsoring LRI." A later negotiation resulted in purchase of equipment and other capital assets by Femcor for another $100,000. This latter sum funded expansion of Northup Library.

The success of Femcor eventually led to its purchase by the Hewlett-Packard Corporation in 1975. The future of LRI itself, however, remained unsettled. For two years, Dyke continued as its director while also serving as chief executive officer of Femcor. His initial suggestion that Femcor hold a

controlling majority on the LRI board failed with the Linfield trustees. At the same time, the science faculty began articulating a vision of basic research that better fit within a liberal arts mission than Dyke's emphasis on applied research. Dr. Drannan Hamby became LRI's head in 1962 with the responsibility for orchestrating its revised agenda.

With their respective realms now more distinctly defined, Dillin and Dyke once again found common ground on behalf of Linfield. Both staunchly advocated Christian education; indeed, the phrase "Training for Christian Democracy" became the unifying motto of the college in the 1950s and early 1960s. Like his father, Dyke joined the board of trustees and became a generous benefactor to his alma mater. Over the course of the turbulent 1960s, however, his strong stances against student activism and intellectual radicalism temporarily alienated him from the college.

1955, Left to right: Dr. Walter Dyke, Board of Trustees Chairman Dr. Hugh Dowd, and President Dillin discuss articles of incorporation for the Linfield Research Institute.

Dillin continued to believe that promoting Christian character in the faculty held the key to recruiting more students, and he strove to enhance the Baptist presence at the college by serving as president of the Oregon State Baptist Convention. Initially his strategies worked but the times ultimately subverted his plan. By the 1960s, fewer students of any denomination chose a college based on its religious affiliation, as academic rigor and social commitment became more central to their calculations. At the same time, the increasingly national character of faculty recruitment brought applications from individuals who would never have considered Linfield in the past. Accordingly Dillin informed the trustees in 1962 that he had "prayerfully" concluded the college might benefit from the presence of faculty members other than "Evangelical Protestants." Roman Catholics and Jews now became eligible for teaching posts so long as they expressed "sympathy with and support [for] the educational purposes of Linfield College."

The intercollegiate athletic program consolidated under Henry Lever blossomed throughout the Dillin years. From 1941 until 1980, Hal Smith coached three sports while also teaching. Roy Helser's baseball teams won fourteen conference

Connecting Community
Going National

1970s, A Homecoming celebration to roil the college's founders

"The Linfield Experience" for roughly one-third of contemporary students includes membership in a fraternity or sorority. Today, we assume these organizations feature Greek letters and dedicate themselves primarily to social aims. It was not always so.

Linfield's antecedents of the Greek system included the Philergian Society, founded in 1874, and The Nicaian Society, founded in 1878. The Philergians dedicated themselves to "the literary, logical and rhetorical culture of its members." The Nicaians advanced "such Literary Attainments as Debating, Elocution and Composition." Both organizations played with classical languages to concoct their titles—the Philergians were "lovers of energy"; the Nicaians harkened back to the Emperor Constantine's fourth-century Council of Nicaea. Some of their debating topics were playful ("Resolved: that the cow is more useful than the horse") and some serious ("Resolved: that the Indians have not been rightly paid for their land"), but all such debates provided high entertainment on Saturday nights. Onlookers included presidents (often as adjudicators), faculty members, and townspeople.

By the early 1900s, college societies steered either toward social life (the Adelphic Society) or service (Daughters of Tradition—D.O.T.s). The Adelphic Society soon adopted a Greek-letter name, Phi Epsilon. As with the other early Greek-letter organizations, Phi Epsilon remained local for nearly a half century. No fan of fraternities, President Leonard Riley established a firm policy against national affiliation. Riley did countenance the first local sorority, Sigma Kappa Phi, in 1924.

The Associated Students of Linfield College in 1946 conducted a poll on national affiliation. For weeks, *The Linfield Review* printed letters for and against the proposal. Lorraine Gilmer wrote, "We speak of traditions, customs, and conventionality that belong to Linfield, but a more apropos word would be 'narrowness.'. . . We must broaden our scope and nationalization would be a big step in that direction." Paul Koch countered, "The institution of nationals would mean just one or two things—erection of social barriers and disruption of social and student government." The ballot on national affiliation went down to defeat by a vote of 135 to 48.

Still the issue did not die. In 1947, the trustees permitted the D.O.T.s to affiliate nationally with and change their name to SPURS, an acronym for Service, Patriotism, Unity, Responsibility, and Sacrifice. This step intensified the campaign to allow national partners for social organizations. On December 3, 1949, the local Alpha Gamma Nu became Linfield's first national Greek-letter organization, changing its name to Theta Chi. In 1950 the local Omega Iota Mu affiliated with Pi Kappa Alpha, and the local Tau Delta Sigma became Phi Sigma Kappa. In 1952 Phi Epsilon became Alpha Tau Omega.

Alarmed that some national fraternities restricted membership on racial grounds, the faculty passed a resolution in 1958 demanding that each Greek-letter organization report its progress toward integration. Any national reporting a racially exclusionist policy was to be barred from campus. The trustees readily adopted this policy.

To this day, one Linfield sorority, Sigma Kappa Phi, and one fraternity, Delta Psi Delta, remain exclusively local. Three other sororities and three present-day fraternities have national affiliations.

1970s, Steve Thomas among his beloved rhododendrons

Connecting Life
Linfield's Clean Geometer

Visitors to Linfield College invariably remark on its attractive grounds. These received their main shape during the presidency of Leonard Riley, who hired New York's John Charles Olmsted to outline a master plan that, twenty years later, was finalized by Samuel Lancaster, builder and landscape architect for the Columbia Highway, and J.C. Compton, a trustee and subsequent recipient of an honorary degree. To many generations of students and faculty, however, Steve Thomas, a 1948 biology graduate who oversaw groundskeeping for twenty-nine years, embodied the college's dedication to its natural beauty.

In 1943, the McMinnville Garden Club hit on the idea of planting a dogwood tree in honor of each year's May Queen. This grand idea soon inspired another from Professor Ralph Storey— why not plant, retrospectively, one dogwood for each previous May Queen, back to 1904? Someone had to keep records and plant those trees. Someone, too, had to research the history of May Day and contact far-flung families of former queens

with pleas for a donation, as the grounds budget did not expand for this cause.

Steve Thomas, then a student working for the grounds crew, assumed these responsibilities— and many more.

Dozens of the mature plantings on campus in the twenty-first century owe their placement to Steve Thomas or one of his own student workers. He specialized in developing new varieties of rhododendron, winning several Best in Class awards from the American Rhododendron Society. Many of his hybrids remain in cultivation, blossoming each spring to evoke reminders that nurturance and renewal serve as constants in education as in nature.

Steve Thomas died in October 1977 from injuries suffered in a fall while pruning a maple tree on campus. A small garden adjacent to Campbell Hall contains a dedicatory plaque in his honor. Professor William I. Elliot of the English department composed this tribute to him:

> He invented Linfield's clean geometry . . .
>
> Nature never had a better teacher.
> His instruments cut exceeding fine
> And at any point on campus
> We always knew just where we stood:
> In the midst of Steve Thomas.
> Wherever we turn, he is here.

championships and in 1966 earned the college's first national championship in any sport. Helser also coached the men's basketball team to four conference championships, one earned with Paul Durham as co-head coach. Durham led football to seven conference titles and two appearances in the National Association of Intercollegiate Athletics (NAIA) playoffs. In twenty years as men's basketball coach, Ted Wilson won a remarkable ten conference titles. His most notable year came in the 1966-67 season, when he suspended all but three varsity players for disciplinary reasons and then coached an assemblage of junior varsity and intramural players to the conference crown. Jane McIlroy built women's intercollegiate athletics from scratch, coaching teams to conference championships in basketball, field hockey, tennis, track and field, and volleyball (see "Coaching as Teaching," p. 126).

The student profile over the course of the twenty-five-year Dillin presidency ran the gamut from older returning World War II veterans studying on the G.I. Bill to the traditional eighteen- to twenty-two-year-olds who populated classrooms and dormitories in the late 1950s and 1960s. By the end of his tenure the postwar baby boom leveled off, introducing renewed challenges to student recruitment and a return to negative balances in the college's annual operating budget.

In fall 1966, Linfield enrolled a record class of 444 freshmen. By fall 1968, immediately following Dillin's retirement, the number of freshmen dropped to 384, including thirty who would not have been admitted under the standards applied two years earlier. Other private colleges of the era struggled with similar problems based on changing national demographics: alongside a leveling off in the raw numbers of traditional college-age students, competition intensified, especially from dramatically expanding community college systems. Moreover, significant inflationary pressure eroded the value of the dollar and raised the costs of higher education.

At various times throughout his presidency, Dillin had broached the subject of resignation or retirement with the Executive Committee or board chairmen. After receiving the predictable protest, Dillin always agreed to stay on, throwing himself into yet another building project. By 1966, however, the talk of retirement became more frequent and more serious. In that year, Governor Mark Hatfield was offered the Linfield presidency as part of a plan whereby Dillin would announce his retirement if Hatfield accepted the board's invitation. Although private communications had suggested that the governor might be receptive, he instead announced plans to run for the U.S. Senate. Chairman Marshall Dana implored Dillin one last time to remain at the helm. He did, but without the same passion for the job.

In 1968, as the final signature act of his presidency, Dillin persuaded the trustees to incur more debt for residence hall construction and to consolidate earlier debts within the building fund into a single note held by U.S. National Bank. Though graduating larger classes than it was recruiting, Linfield continued to expand dormitory capacity. No records survive to suggest that the board discussed at any length the future enrollment challenges facing private colleges.

Little in the Dillin legacy positioned the college to respond to new conditions. Save for the addition of several new majors, the curriculum had taken shape during Elam Anderson's presidency and needed reform by the 1960s. The effort to grow the Baptist student population had focused recruitment efforts on a pool that was shrinking, due both to demographics and to the continued schism among regional Baptist associations. The comfortable and picturesque campus concealed an underlying fiscal vulnerability. Total endowment grew from $923,934 in 1943 to only $1,767,748 in 1968. When adjusted for inflation over that period, this latter sum constituted a net loss in real terms of $91,000. Thanks to Dillin's history of sound financial management in the 1930s, the trustees deferred to him in investment decisions, with no input from professional advisors. Most outside contributions, as with the Femcor settlement, supported the building program. Incurring debt for expansion had been wise and necessary at the outset of Dillin's presidency, but

Right: *1960s, Two students inside the observatory*

Dr. William R. Frerichs

Dr. Jonas A. "Steine" Jonasson

Connecting Learning
Servant Historians

Presidents Truman Brownson and Leonard Riley took particular pains to research and write historically about the college they served. Two faculty members and academic deans also recorded pieces of Linfield's story even as they themselves helped to shape it.

William R. Frerichs, a native of Germany who graduated from Carthage College and Colgate-Rochester Theological Seminary, came to McMinnville College in 1912 to teach German and Greek. During World War I, students refused to take his German classes, and some townspeople agitated against him. Frerichs expressed gratitude on more than one occasion that his faculty colleagues stood staunchly beside him during this difficult time.

Over his years at the college Frerichs wore many hats. As librarian and editor of college publications, he wrote extensively about Linfield. In 1928 he replaced Emanuel Northup as faculty dean. After completing his doctorate at the University of Griefswald, Germany, during a leave of absence in 1930-31, he returned to become acting president. When Elam Anderson assumed that role in 1932, Frerichs reverted to his multiple roles of dean, director of publications, and teacher until his retirement in 1941.

Frerichs continued to serve even while retired. He tried his hand at translating into German some of Walter Dyke's papers on field emissions theory, but when he rendered the English term "field strength" into the German equivalent of "meadow power," he ended his brief foray beyond the humanities.

Frerichs remains the only person to have his name bestowed on two separate college structures: a fine arts building destroyed by fire in 1969 and a residence hall dedicated in 1979.

Jonas A. "Steine" Jonasson, the son of Icelandic immigrants, hailed originally from South Dakota but as a youth moved to Burlington, Washington. He arrived in McMinnville as a student in fall 1922, joining the first class to matriculate under the new college name—Linfield. After receiving his BA degree in social science in 1926, he went on to earn an MA in history from the University of Washington and a PhD in history from Stanford University. Upon returning to Linfield in 1931 as a faculty member, Jonasson chaired the history department until his retirement in 1969. He also served several stints as dean of administration.

Teaching courses in both history and political science, Jonasson took a keen interest in combining theory and practice by writing about the communities he knew firsthand. In 1938, he published *Bricks Without Straw*, Linfield College's definitive history to that time. He followed in 1957 with three chapters in *A History of the United States Air Force, 1907-1957*, based on his experience as an instructor in the Army Air Corps. In 1967, he concluded with *100 Years of Witnessing*, a history of his beloved McMinnville First Baptist Church.

Through it all, Jonasson remained an inspiring teacher. J. Richard Nokes—alumnus from the class of 1935, trustee, and longtime editor of the *Oregonian*—paid tribute to Jonasson's legacy: "He is a man that not only taught his subject, history, but made his students think. He was my major professor, and my favorite." The history department continues to honor his memory through the Steine Jonasson lecture series, which brings outstanding history scholars to campus to speak about their research.

proved imprudent at the end. The next president faced repayment of a consolidated $976,000 bond on residence halls that could not generate the revenue to service that debt. What is more, social upheavals associated with the civil rights movement and Vietnam War affected students and faculty alike, rendering them less docile than customary. Any energy he might have had to address such matters disappeared when Dillin suffered whiplash in a 1967 auto accident, precipitating a desire to retire that, this time, the trustees had to accept.

A Controversial and Transitional President

President Dillin's resignation letter of October 27, 1967, named his departure date as June 1, 1968. A small trustee committee reviewed the credentials of thirty candidates and invited four (two of them from the faculty) to interview with a few senior faculty members and other trustees. When no consensus emerged, Dean Winthrop Dolan was invited on May 25, 1968, to serve as acting president. His tenure was short, for trustee and search committee chairman Harry Prior then nominated Dr. Gordon C. Bjork, a distinguished economist at the Columbia University School of Business, former member of the First Baptist Church of Seattle, and the great-nephew of Elam Anderson. Prior and board chairman Philip Renshaw interviewed Bjork in June, initially thinking him too young for the post. However, Bjork's constructive views on how to deal with student unrest, forged at Columbia in tumultuous times, impressed both men. A Rhodes Scholar with an AB from Dartmouth College, an MA from Oxford, and a PhD from the University of Washington, Bjork brought academic credentials that impressed the senior faculty. They recommended him to the Executive Committee, which endorsed the nomination and called for a special meeting of the full board on July 20. There it was voted "unanimously and enthusiastically, that Dr. Gordon C. Bjork be elected President of the College."

The contrast between Bjork and Dillin was dramatic. Even Dillin's supporters referred to him as a "benign dictator." In contrast, since faculty governance scarcely existed when he arrived at the helm, Bjork moved quickly to create a Rank and Tenure Committee to advise the president and trustees formally on faculty advancement. Such empowerment of the faculty paid dividends in revitalizing the liberal arts emphasis and attracting grants to sponsor a high-profile array of campus speakers. A livelier public engagement with the life of the mind became a staple of college activity, in sharp contrast with the intellectual traditionalism of the Dillin era.

The 32-year-old president made a favorable impression among students. He wore his hair fashionably long and did not hesitate to appear among them without his coat and tie. Due to his emphasis on racially diversifying the student body, the highest proportion of black Linfield alumni graduated during Bjork's presidency. In fall 1969 alone, twenty-five African Americans enrolled at Linfield, their presence made possible by federal financial aid that the college had not previously tapped. Also in keeping with the times, Bjork defended peaceful student protest, promoted student autonomy, and liberalized outmoded policies of student conduct such as imposed residence hall hours for women only. During his first year, the faculty—at the urging of the college chaplain, Joseph Ban—abolished mandatory student attendance at convocation, the last vestige of the required chapel that had been a defining feature of "The Linfield Experience" for previous generations of alumni.

As at many other private colleges throughout the country, the enrollment surge of the early and mid-1960s had caused an overexpansion of staff and facilities at Linfield. The operating budget for 1968-69 (authorized by the trustees under Dillin) had increased faculty and staff salaries across the board by 5 percent without raising tuition, fees, or room charges. When enrollment fell below projected levels that fall, the college ran a substantial operating deficit in Bjork's first year. Despite dramatic cuts in janitorial, maintenance,

Right: *1968, Susan Bjork, Gordon Bjork, president, 1968 to 1974;* front, *daughter Hannah;* left to right, *daughters Katie and Becky*

and secretarial staff, Bjork could not rein in the budget.

The most recent audit letter from the accounting firm responsible for review of college finances criticized many financial operations, including management of the endowment. In response, the trustees appointed their own committee to oversee investments, removing Harry Dillin from the singular role he had played with respect to the endowment since the mid-1930s. This step soured initially cordial relations between Bjork and Dillin, who had retired to a new home in McMinnville.

Believing that Linfield's difficulties could not be solved by incremental means, Bjork urged the trustees to focus on the essential fact that too many private colleges chased fewer students as public higher education increasingly offered a more affordable option. To compete, he argued, Linfield needed to distinguish itself academically and adapt to a permanently changed student marketplace.

As he sought to contend with inherited structural issues of management and overexpansion, in his first year Bjork also confronted the rising tide of protest over the Vietnam War. He espoused the power of free, full, and open debate in a public educational forum to defuse tension and generate light rather than heat. This new emphasis on academic freedom predictably fostered unprecedented faculty and student outspokenness. Faculty members James Duke, Vincil Jacobs, and William Elliot, with student assistance, published an underground newspaper, BARBQ, which trustee Walter Dyke deemed sufficiently "inflammatory" to require a "law and order" response from the president and trustees. Though Bjork remonstrated with the faculty members responsible for the publication, he defended their right to express their views.

Dyke's sensitivities derived in part from rumors that Femcor, holder of many military contracts, had been targeted for a student demonstration (which never materialized). He, like many Americans, had concluded that the violence surrounding the 1968 Democratic Convention in Chicago meant that revolution did indeed threaten the nation. Dyke's letters to fellow trustees regularly included articles about protest elsewhere,

with little information specific to Linfield itself. In the May 1969 trustee meeting, Dyke proposed a special investigating committee to expose radicals in the faculty and student body. He resigned from the board when it rejected his proposal. An attempted mediation between Dyke and Bjork failed when Bjork told the trustees he found such a committee unacceptable and Dyke announced he wanted nothing more to do with an institution that harbored anarchists.

In fact, the activism at Linfield remained mild in comparison to colleges and universities in the East and in California. Writing of the protest held at Linfield as part of the nationwide October 15, 1969, Vietnam Moratorium, James Hitchman observes, "It was all very friendly and unlike the repetitious outbreaks disturbing many other campuses." Nonetheless, Bjork's standing in the local community began to suffer. It didn't help that Dick Gregory and Jerry Rubin, both radical political leaders of the era, came to speak at Linfield by student invitation during Bjork's second year. Many in the community found such controversial speakers unsavory, while failing to observe how tepidly Linfield students responded to their message. Not so Hitchman, whose study of *Liberal Arts Colleges in Oregon and Washington* notes drolly: "Linfield took it all in stride; Rubin's statement that college was a mental prison and prolonged nursery was juxtaposed [in the student newspaper] with pictures of the Homecoming Queen and her court." All during the campus unrest, no classes were cancelled nor windows broken.

This heightened engagement with the realities beyond the campus paralleled equally aggressive curricular modernization. Bjork increased library holdings by 40 percent, persuaded the faculty to replace its longstanding core general education curriculum with a distributional model encouraging interdisciplinary teaching, and spurred environmental awareness with both new environmental science courses and a major grant-supported conference entitled "Man and Land." By scheduling classes in five-credit blocks, he hoped to immerse students more deeply in the course material and encourage faculty to cross disciplinary boundaries within

Early 1970s, President Bjork at a podium

Lincabin, the college's retreat on the edge of the Three Sisters Wilderness, before fire destroyed it in 2006

1973 Homecoming Queen Serita Williams and Billy Scott

their syllabi. Merit scholarships raised the profile of incoming classes while fewer probationary students received admission. This emphasis on Linfield's growing academic reputation bore fruit: despite a slight overall decrease in the total number of students enrolling in regional colleges between 1970 and 1972, Linfield increased its freshman numbers from 368 to 429.

Cocurricular environmental education expanded with programs at the Sitka Center at Cascade Head. Thanks to a gift of leased land and to materials provided by Brooks-Scanlon Inc., Lincabin would later (1975) be built near Sisters, Oregon, to host college outdoor enthusiasts. In addition, Bjork launched the Upward Bound program to foster college-track preparation for disadvantaged local youth. The first student and faculty trustees came onto the board thanks to bylaw changes that the president advocated. Alcohol was permitted on campus in keeping with state law, a further step away from the in loco parentis philosophy of student life maintained throughout the Dillin era. Alumni witnessed a dramatic change in *The Linfield College Bulletin,* which devoted several issues to controversial themes and allowed students to publish their thoughts to the larger Linfield community in ways never before countenanced (see "Jocks vs. Longhairs," p. 113). *Linews,* the newly named student newspaper, published an editorial on flag burning that many regarded as unpatriotic.

(see "Jocks vs. Longhairs," p. 113)

Connecting Learning
Contesting a Legacy

Like the college it revitalized, Frances Ross Linfield's gift to McMinnville College resulted from years of frugality and foresight rather than inherited wealth. During her marriage, she and her husband chose to live on a single salary, alternating each year as to whose would suffice. They invested their unspent income and resolved to devote their savings to Christian education.

After George Fisher Linfield died in 1890, his widow expanded her business holdings in Spokane, Washington, though some acquisitions fell to her unsought. Spokane auditors' records indicate that in 1894 title was transferred to her on land owned by her parents, who could no longer manage the payments on it, in exchange for her assumption of the mortgage and tax liability.

Mrs. Linfield acquired her most desirable property near the elegant Davenport Hotel in 1916 from the Ross Holding Company. Along with other family members, she served as a company trustee for additional properties acquired from her parents along with some acquired by her brother, Edward Sherman Ross.

The Linfield gift to McMinnville College was privately contested as soon as it became public. Relatives of her two brothers wrote many letters to Frances Linfield. A few supported her generosity, but most decried their perceived loss of inheritance. In the transcribed record of a 1923 conversation between President Leonard Riley, Frances Linfield, and G.C. Condon, a Seattle attorney, the claims to the property by George Ross, her younger brother, were delicately raised and determinedly rejected.

Even so, the matter did not end. A year after her death in 1940, Frances Linfield's bequest was challenged in federal district court by the heirs of Edward Ross. The suit alleged that the 1916 transfer from the Ross Holding Company to Mrs. Linfield constituted a fraud. The court in 1941 declared the suit untimely, for twenty-eight years had elapsed between the bequest in 1922 and the plaintiff's date of filing. Although no ruling ensued on the case's merits, the court took great pains to reject in writing all five of the plaintiff's grounds for alleging fraud. Presiding Judge L.B. Schwellenbach characterized the suit rather directly:

> It is apparent to me that Mrs. Linfield occupied that most unfortunate of positions—she was the family leader and favorite to whom all of the relatives looked for advice and assistance and whose fortune they secretly hoped to inherit upon her death. Any person occupying this position must brave the most vigorous wrath when he decides that the time has come in his life to cut loose from the ties of such family responsibility.

Far from revealing any abandonment of "family responsibility," the record shows that Frances Linfield regularly sent money to her blood relatives. Through the terms of her bequest to Linfield, she also provided scholarships for her nieces and nephews. Given such largesse, the judge's incredulity over the suit seems reasonable.

1922, Frances Ross Linfield's contested property, West Sprague Avenue and North Monroe Street, Spokane, Washington

Roy Beadle

Connecting Community
A Quiet Voice of Reason

Chosen for their wisdom, faith, or financial means, trustees often toil with little public recognition from the various constituencies they serve. Sometimes the attention they do receive takes aim at their governing decisions, which necessarily weigh future interests against present needs. To most college citizens, the latter regularly weigh more heavily than the former.

The names of several board chairmen and trustees grace various spots on campus in recognition of their financial support of the college. But gifts of talent have been equally essential in assuring Linfield's longevity.

As longtime board secretary, Roy Beadle led in a quiet way that may well have saved the college. A 1934 Linfield graduate, Beadle served as a trustee for forty-three years (1947 to 1990). As a journalist and longtime editorial page editor for the *Oregon Journal*, he lacked the means to

Congresswoman Edith Green

become a major financial contributor, but his wordsmith's skills proved vital during the tumult of the late 1960s and early 1970s, when the fevered pitch of the times led a few members in each college constituency—trustees, administration, faculty, students, and alumni—to place personal agendas above the interests of the college.

In his steady and unifying voice, Roy Beadle wrote letters behind the scenes to those who, in his judgment, favored rashness over reason. He sought valiantly but unsuccessfully to persuade Walter Dyke and Hugh Dowd to remain members of the board—and pleaded that they be fair in their criticisms after they had left. He wrote the editors of BARBQ and *Linews*, remonstrating with them for their stridency, while publicly defending their right to free expression. Forceful when necessary, he never condescended. Perhaps his greatest contribution lay in persuading Congresswoman Edith Green to remain on the Board of Trustees. "Disillusioned . . . with the verbal clashes and attacks on individuals rather than discussions of issues," she had sought to resign following her first board meeting in 1970, but Beadle encouraged her to rethink her course of action. Her retention proved crucial to the institution's public credibility during a difficult period.

Uncelebrated at the time and without flash or self-aggrandizement, Roy Beadle demonstrated for Congresswoman Green and many other Linfield supporters that promoting quality education requires equal measures of tough-mindedness and mutual respect: effective civil discourse requires no less in any venue.

Such changes provoked considerable backlash, including among trustees. When Bjork inserted a phrase into the masthead of *Linews* clarifying that the students spoke for themselves, not for the college, some disaffected trustees saw it as further evidence of undue permissiveness. By the end of Bjork's second academic year, five additional board members, including former chairman and long-time athletics booster Dr. Hugh Dowd, resigned in protest. Dowd's departure fueled a public perception that the new president devalued the sports program, as noted by the *Oregon Journal*. Emphasis on new merit scholarships based on standardized test scores, rather than on athletic scholarships, fed this fear, though it subsided when Ad Rutschman's 1971 baseball team won the NAIA national championship.

A worsening financial picture compounded the young president's troubles. Bjork's investment in the academic program drew only partially on grants and contributions to the college. To bring in added students, financial aid expenditures exceeded the budget. The operating deficit grew and the building debt could not be covered, forcing Bjork to seek a $500,000 loan from U.S. National Bank. The board also authorized a $300,000 loan from the endowment (at 11 percent interest) to manage the deficit. They likewise approved taking proceeds from capital gains and applying a portion to the annual budget, a move that backfired in the deep stock market decline of 1973-74.

Faced with these challenges, Bjork argued for dramatic fiscal changes to accompany the sweeping changes in curriculum and student life he had fostered. A 1971 plan (never implemented) proposed that Linfield entirely eliminate the financial aid discount on tuition. By dropping tuition from $1,800 to $1,000, Bjork argued, the college could secure many more matriculants. The college would then invite their parents to sign a "covenant" agreeing that, if they remained satisfied with their offspring's education, they would contribute 2 percent per year of taxable income during the course of the child's enrollment. Graduating students would enter into a similar covenant to contribute 1 percent of taxable income per year so long as they felt benefited by their Linfield education.

Such daring earned Bjork sufficient respect from the trustees to turn around the internal dissent generated by his first two years as president. With their support he pursued a transformative agenda. The daunting challenges facing a meagerly endowed, tuition-dependent college in a time of protest and hyperinflation could perhaps have been met by conservative steps to cut expenses immediately and by reliance on the college's traditional constituencies to see it through. In hiring Bjork, however, the trustees had precluded such responses. They steadfastly joined him in the search for new constituencies and new revenues.

A second Linfield Plan took shape, and on May 31, 1973, Bjork delivered to the trustees and college community a sixteen-page special report. The idea of a significant discount in tuition reappeared but in a radically different form. Bjork had diagnosed one structural problem facing higher education as underutilization of facilities. Though paying for building and grounds maintenance year-round, the campus only generated revenue for nine months. Bjork proposed a twelve-month block-scheduling plan to complement the existing block plan for five-credit classes. As an incentive to enroll across the year, students would receive discounts on both tuition and housing for the summer. Faculty could either spread out their teaching loads over the full year or earn a supplement for increased summer teaching.

In advocating the Linfield Plan, however, Bjork had to contend with resistance from the newly empowered faculty, whose growing influence he himself had fostered. As the critical state of the college's finances became more widely known, some faculty agreed with community members that Bjork's perceived arrogance undermined his effectiveness. Concern that his ideas were too numerous and his follow-through too lax also eroded confidence in his vision for the institution. Clashes multiplied and wounds festered.

The faculty debated the Linfield Plan during the fall of 1973, eventually approving a block schedule–two semesters, a winter term, and two summer terms–with 63 percent in favor.

During the debate Bjork suggested to the faculty that defeat of the plan would prompt him to seek other employment. Justifying this tactic to a skeptical trustee, Bjork explained he "felt he had to take strong action to impress the faculty with the importance of making decisions and preparing for the future."

Bjork's faith in the Linfield Plan rested on the belief that its flexibility would attract sufficient numbers of students to protect the planned 1974-75 budget from additional cuts. (The president and trustees had already decided against salary increases for the coming year.) Unfortunately, financial conditions worsened. The imposition of quotas by foreign oil suppliers in 1973-74 led to a steep recession, a higher rate of inflation, and gasoline rationing throughout the country. In the first three months of 1973, the value of Linfield's endowment fell from $1.7 million to $1.1 million. Moreover, nearly a third of the endowment was now encumbered by the debt owed on the earlier internal loan of $300,000, and U.S. National Bank refused to extend its credit line further. Linfield's accumulated deficit thus threatened to exceed its liquid assets. Not since Riley's ascension to the presidency in 1906 had the college balance sheet looked so grim.

The trustees approved the Linfield Plan at a special meeting on November 17, 1973. Their resolution mandating a balanced 1974-75 budget required Bjork to enact substantial operating budget reductions after he had already sacrificed considerable faculty goodwill over the Linfield Plan. Two specific measures heightened tensions around budget planning. Contingency contracts forecast employee salary cuts of up to 20 percent (1 percent for each $10,000 of projected shortfall). Another step proposed the elimination of faculty positions and even of majors in philosophy, religion, and modern languages. Basing the rationale for these cuts on low enrollments, Bjork now seemed guilty of betraying the very liberal arts environment he had earlier championed, with the result that former allies bitterly dropped away.

Faculty restiveness peaked at the March 7, 1974, meeting of the Faculty Assembly when a group of faculty members introduced a vote of no confidence against Bjork based on six key failures. Though some had seen the charges beforehand, many had not. In any case, the bill of allegations did not follow the assembly's own rules for promulgating faculty business. Bjork learned of the proposal only two hours before the meeting and had no opportunity to respond in writing to the charges. During debate, some faculty members proposed that the motion be tabled to allow more time for consideration, but Bjork himself objected. He wanted an immediate decision, declaring his intention to resign if the vote went against him. Judging by those who offered opinions on the floor of the assembly, sentiment seemed to run in the president's favor, though most of those who spoke confined their remarks to decrying the means employed by Bjork's opponents. Still, the actual tally favored the no-confidence position by a thirty-six to thirty margin. Those in favor had felt little need to speak, having determined the strength of their numbers beforehand. Ironically, the free speech rights of several of the opposition leaders had been staunchly defended to the trustees only nine months into Bjork's presidency.

Bjork resigned in a letter to the trustee Executive Committee dated March 8. The trustees, however, feared that accepting his resignation outright would seem to endorse the events leading up to it. In short order, the student government passed a resolution in support of the president, also decrying the means used by the faculty opposition, which had, in their view, ignored student opinion entirely. The damage had been done, however: the trustees could not reassemble the broken shell of Bjork's presidency. The Executive Committee met on March 31 and April 1 to pass two resolutions. In the first, the board decided "not to accept the resignation of President Bjork dated March 8, 1974" and to "reject the 'no confidence' resolution passed by the faculty on March 7, 1974." In the second, it accepted "with deep regret" a new letter of resignation from Bjork dated April 1, 1974, with an effective date of May 31, 1974.

President Gordon Bjork's legacy remains a strongly divided one with emphatic positives and negatives. Many of his initiatives moved Linfield from a complacent parochialism into full partnership with other modern colleges and universities. At most quality private institutions regionally and nationally, founding sectarian perspectives had yielded much earlier to a nonsectarian emphasis on social responsibility, inclusiveness, and growing internationalism. Though Linfield came late to these perspectives, Bjork undeniably served as their catalyst. What is more, some of his changes have become familiar features of today's Linfield, including the popular January Term program, the practice of shared governance between faculty and administration, and the extensive degree of student autonomy.

Yet Bjork's initiatives undeniably came at a substantial cost. The college community became split and fearful, while members of the local community remained antagonistic to many of the campus changes they had witnessed. Bjork had reversed the enrollment decline but had not been able to address accumulating deficits. However the blame is apportioned between unsound financial management and sustained negative economic trends beyond anyone's control, the college exited Bjork's presidency with little more than the value of its physical plant weighing on the positive side of its balance sheet. Though the threat facing the college proved not as great as in 1906, there were no guarantees of Linfield's survival.

For a second time Dr. Winthrop Dolan became acting president. With ample reason to be pessimistic, college supporters clung to a few signs of hope. Within the Linfield faculty itself, Dr. John Day, professor of physics, advocated a foray into adult education as a means of stabilizing Linfield's budget—an area that Bjork, too, had foreseen as critical to institutional survival but had done little to pursue. Linfield's initial step toward nontraditional undergraduate education took the form of a partnership with Good Samaritan Hospital whereby diploma-program nurses would have the opportunity to earn a BA degree. A parallel story from Oregon's pioneer past thus began to converge with Linfield's own story. ∎

Did you know?

…that the Young Men's Christian Association (1887) and Young Women's Christian Association (1887) not only predated but also gave rise to the Associated Students of McMinnville College, formed in 1903.

…that The Baptist College at McMinnville officially changed its name on June 16, 1898, to McMinnville College.

…that a vote of the student body in 1924 favored adopting the Wildcat as mascot because Linfield was "a small school with a lot of fight and scratch."

…that had a Chicago industrialist, owner of the Kimball Music Company, donated $100,000 in the late 1910s, Linfield College might today be named Conway College.

…that the college adopted its present school colors, properly Cardinal and Purple, in 1917.

…that before 1924, spectators at athletic events cheered variously for the "Baptists" or the "Cardinal and Purple."

…that Dr. and Mrs. Leonard Riley's ashes lie buried outside the north-facing window of the president's office in Melrose Hall.

…that world-renowned mime Marcel Marceau *spoke* at Linfield's 1973 commencement.

…that today's "Observatory," relocated in the 1950s from near Pioneer Hall to Linfield's then south boundary, serves as a convenience store in the center of campus.

…that Merle Templeton, class of 1974, was the first male to be admitted to and graduated from the Good Samaritan School of Nursing.

…that President Charles U. Walker's middle name is Urmston.

…that Irene (Hartman) Dillin, wife of President Harry Dillin (1943 to 1968), was May Queen in 1939.

…that the "A" in President Vivian A. Bull's name stands for the ever-popular Ann.

…that fans of *The Simpsons* (television's longest running prime time comedy and animated series) may thank alumni Homer and Margaret (Wiggum) Groening (both class of 1941) for son Matt's inspired creations Homer and Marge Simpson. Homer Groening (above middle) received a Distinguished Flying Cross in World War II and later became a prominent filmmaker. Among her many satisfying accomplishments in life, Margaret was chosen Linfield's May Queen (Margaret III) in 1941 (see photo, p. 64)

For Trivia Buffs

The Parallel Story

As President Mark Bailey strove to define higher standards for the Baptist-affiliated McMinnville College in the mid-1870s, the Episcopal community in Portland undertook the founding of Good Samaritan Hospital. For a story that unfolds alongside, offers striking parallels to, and then merges with that of Linfield College, one must turn back once again to the nineteenth century.

Organizing their first services in 1839, Episcopalians antedated the Baptists in Oregon by a scant five years. Both denominations found pioneer soil hard digging, and not until 1853 did the Episcopal Church designate a missionary bishop, Thomas Fielding Scott, for the Oregon Territory. Few records of Scott's time in Oregon have survived, though a will drawn up before he returned to his New York home indicates that he left Oregon in 1867. He must have laid a promising foundation, judging by the achievements of his successor, Bishop Wistar Morris, who arrived from Pennsylvania in 1869. Morris quickly launched a fund-raising campaign for Good Samaritan Hospital, the most ambitious program among several that marked his productive service to the region. By the time of his death in 1906, Morris had also founded numerous parishes, St. Helen's Hall (then a girl's school, now the coed Oregon Episcopal School), Bishop Scott Academy (a boy's school, now defunct), and a Chinese Mission School (also gone).

In part, Morris drew energy from the swaggering character of 1870s Portland itself. Incorporated in 1852, the city had grown from 2,917 citizens in 1860 to 9,565 by decade's end, in great part because of its role as a supply depot for those pursuing their fortunes in the California Gold Rush. Buoyed by the resultant prosperity enjoyed in Oregon and Washington, Morris's hopes for a new hospital prompted the first advertising solicitation in early 1873 and purchase of the necessary land on October 18 of the same year. Henry Failing, a Baptist already familiar to the trustees of McMinnville College, became an early subscriber to the Episcopal project —evidence of the urgently felt need for a Protestant alternative to the Catholics' St. Vincent Hospital, which opened only a few months before Good Samaritan. Otherwise, only a mental asylum that sometimes doubled as a hospital served Portlanders needing overnight medical care.

As his building site, Morris purchased from Dr. Rodney Glisan four and one-half acres of "brush and briar" amidst "the belt of timber which skirts the city." The land lay circumscribed by Twenty-first, Twenty-third, L (now Lovejoy), and N (now Northrup) streets. Architect James Cumming designed an H-shaped wooden building whose two parallel wings would house the hospital and an orphanage (in reality, a home for destitute children, some with living parents unable to care for them).

Given the limited number of Episcopal communicants

Bishop Wistar Morris
Oregon Historical Society CN 012973

Opposite: *1894, Good Samaritan Hospital Nurse Training Program graduating class with Emily Loveridge in black.* Front row, far right: *Lillian Long.* Others in the class: *Gertrude Churchman, Edith Duke, Ellen Dunseath, Marian Eastham, Annie Graham, and Label Lake*

anticipated targets, for the new facility sat at the end of a bumpy and often muddy road far from the city center. Rather than undertake the jarring ride to Twenty-first Street, many potential users visited nearer private dispensaries or patronized itinerant surgeons who operated in rooms rented from city hotels. Even its designation as the official hospital for the Port of Portland could not offset Good Samaritan's accessibility problems. Within a few years the fledgling hospital, newly cut off from downtown Portland by fencing posted around intervening private property, closed for a full year beginning in fall 1878. Road construction dominated the next twelve months, and the facility reopened in 1879, though Bishop Morris lamented "an alarming indebtedness of $636."

Still, the bishop's astute oversight continued to build Good Samaritan's future. It did not hurt that two of the community's most respected physicians, Wilson (the first qualified practitioner to settle permanently in Portland) and Glisan, had also agreed to serve on its inaugural Board of Managers. Robust subscriptions and the quality of treatment furthered the hospital's local reputation. Closing the orphanage in 1883 to make room for more sick beds, Good Samaritan also contracted to care for Portland's indigents at the cost of fifty cents a day.

The Good Samaritan patient ledger for 1882 shows that Portland had already achieved a multinational character. One hundred and six hospital users hailed from the U.S. or Canada, a hundred and three from eleven European countries, three from the West Indies, two from China, and two from Africa. Four were American Indians. As to religion, the patients espoused twelve different Christian denominations, while forty-four had "no religion," thirteen were "of uncertain religion," and two were identified as "heathens."

With the arrival of a female nursing staff, the modern face of Good Samaritan Hospital began to emerge. In 1883 two trained nurses, Sister Mary and Sister Hannah, augmented the staff and unsuccessfully sought to establish a nurses' training program. Despite their failure, they encouraged an

within the bishop's Oregon/Washington jurisdiction (only 704 in 1874), his success seems all the more remarkable. On May 15, 1874 (Ascension Day), nearly 300 Portlanders attended the laying of Good Samaritan's cornerstone. The untroubled construction project allowed the building to open its doors on October 9, 1875, guided by a charter pledging to accept "all [patients] regardless of race, color, creed or religion." Soon thereafter Morris added a stipulation that "one-fourth of its work must go to the poor and needy." Annual reports well into the 1950s show that the hospital kept faith with this mission.

The day after opening its twenty-five beds to patients, Good Samaritan admitted its first occupant: William Smith from nearby Oswego. Others followed, as did orphans to occupy the opposite wing. Before long, all four consulting and attending physicians–Dr. Robert B. Wilson, Dr. Rodney Glisan, Dr. Curtis T. Strong, and Dr. James T. Ghislen–began regularly treating patients. Even so, demand fell below

1883, Emily Loveridge at age twenty-three

institutional vision linking medical care and education that soon produced a successful physicians' intern program. Emma Wakeman assumed the duties of hospital superintendent in 1884. A capable administrator, Wakeman retired the institution's debt and oversaw a series of expansions during her twenty years in office.

Growing Episcopal membership led to Oregon's designation as a formal diocese by 1889, and Morris exchanged his status as missionary prelate for that of bishop proper. In one of his first acts under his new title, he legally incorporated

Good Samaritan. The first board, which he chaired, included two additional clergymen (Rev. Thomas Cole and Rev. William Powell) and two physicians (Dr. Simeon Josephi and Dr. George Wilson). Josephi soon became treasurer, an office he held for over forty years.

Josephi had already established himself as a major player in Portland's medical community. In 1887 he helped launch the University of Oregon Medical School, which remained affiliated with Good Samaritan Hospital until its move to Marquam Hill in 1919. The new program had resulted from a revolt among several Willamette University Medical School physicians who had rallied around Josephi when other colleagues had opposed his return after a leave of absence. Together the rebels petitioned the president of the University of Oregon regents, Judge Matthew Deady, to establish a rival program in Portland. Deady, an original subscriber to Good Samaritan Hospital, supported the request, and brought the other regents with him. The new medical school opened its doors in an abandoned grocery store moved to the corner of Twenty-third and Lovejoy, though clinical instruction occurred at the hospital. Josephi himself served as its first dean, a position he occupied for twenty-five years.

Emily Loveridge Defines Excellence in Nursing Education

With affiliated physician education well under way and fiscal operations stabilized, Wakeman revived plans to establish nursing education at the hospital. In 1890 she hired Emily Loveridge, a graduate of New York City's Bellevue Hospital nursing program, to craft a Portland variant. In the process "Miss Emily" would become a revered Northwest leader in the field until her death in 1941. She had moved to Oregon at the urging of her father, Rev. Daniel E. Loveridge, rector of St. Mary's Episcopal Church in Eugene. Arriving in Portland in April 1890, by June 1 she had recruited six student nurses who met for classes in the evenings after work. An engaging reminiscence of her early years at the hospital through 1909 provides a vivid picture of the trials she and her students

Dr. Robert B. Wilson, Portland's first established physician
Oregon Historical Society CN 021906

Dr. Rodney Glisan, who provided land for Good Samaritan Hospital
Oregon Historical Society CN 0211343

faced in the early days. They endured a daily schedule that few today would tolerate: "We all worked, and no one grumbled, not even at the end of a perfect day of from 12 to 16 hours of labor, for there were no hours off in those days and sometimes no afternoons. The work was hard, the hours long and everybody worked."

Loveridge relentlessly tackled the indifferent hygiene and lack of sterile conditions plaguing hospital practice at the time. When not caring for patients or attending classes, the students scrubbed, cleaned, and even painted. Upon attending her first surgery, Loveridge discovered that physicians had been directed by Wakeman to store sutures in the window shades for greater "convenience." Loveridge halted the practice immediately and used the occasion to teach her students how to weave the sutures into properly sterilized and arranged bandages. The same reformist zeal corrected other unsanitary conditions throughout the hospital.

Loveridge drew her curriculum from her alma mater's commitment to two main precepts espoused by Florence Nightingale herself. The first rested upon acquisition of theoretical and practical knowledge demonstrated by examination. The second emphasized development of sound character through discipline and obedience—though in Emily Loveridge's mind, obedience had only one justification. In forty years of service to Good Samaritan, she insisted that a nurse's discipline reside not simply in following rules, but in the steady and persistent contribution one made to patient welfare. Dr. Harry Carlos DeVighne, who interned at the hospital after Loveridge became its chief administrator, made clear that "Miss Emily, the Superintendent, held to the simple theory that hospitals should be operated with due regard for the comfort and welfare of patients. Therefore she ruled out everything incompatible with that objective." While observing rules usually produced a good result, if blind obedience might endanger a patient, Miss Emily expected her nurses to think their way to a better-informed course of action. She also insisted that a medical practitioner's good character required a healthy dose of humility, a lesson

Opposite: 1913-16, Nursing students in the Good Samaritan kitchen

DeVighne clearly internalized: "We were students, she reminded us. In medical school we had studied human bodies and their diseases. We must now study human lives and learn how to lighten some of their burdens."

Exacting in her enforcement of this professional code, Loveridge inspired loyalty and gratitude among those with whom she worked. Only twenty-nine years old when placed in charge of the upstart program, she tempered her expectations with patience and humor, providing some relief to those expected to meet her demanding standards. As one source put it, "A favorite joke was to ask the nurse in the diet kitchen if she could boil water without burning it." Loveridge roomed at the hospital, a fitting choice for someone who defined her life by her commitment to her work. Her first twelve students all completed the two-year course, adopting as an emblem of graduation a uniform with "a double stripe of blue and white seersucker." Indeed, Miss Emily's keen eye for character and her inspirational example meant that students rarely dropped out or were expelled. Their greatest failing—understandable given their arduous workdays—lay in sometimes yielding to drowsiness during lectures delivered by the physicians who taught their evening courses. Those who began their studies lacking physical stamina soon acquired it by helping orderlies carry stretcher-borne patients up the staircases to their beds. Delivering a blunt corrective by example, Loveridge herself regularly stepped in to lend a hand if anyone shrank from such duty.

Good Samaritan continued to grow and change as the nineteenth century gave way to the twentieth. The first brick addition to the campus was the Lewis Wing, built in 1899. The next year a fire above the men's ward required evacuation of the hospital and could easily have destroyed the whole building had it not been successfully confined to the attic and roof. The nurses, who had been warning about the fire danger posed by straw tick beds, then saw to the purchase of actual mattresses for future patients. A Nurses' Home opened in 1902, and by 1905 a new Northwest Wing housed the Couch Memorial Surgery. When failing health

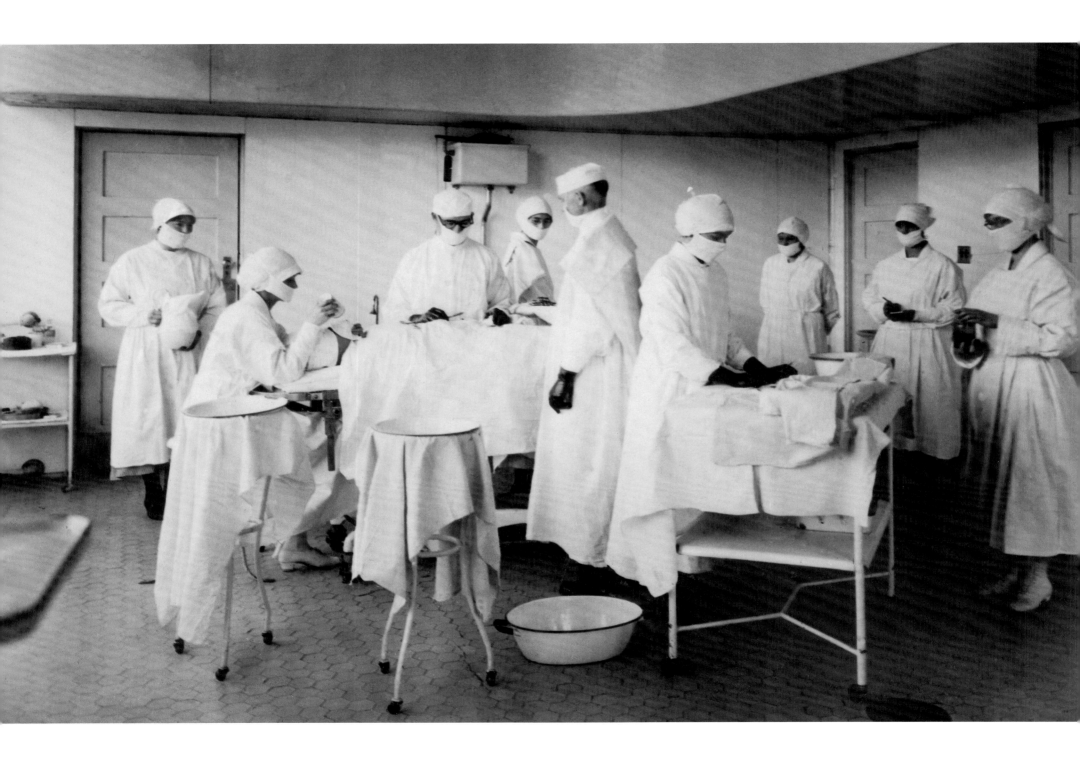

Daddy Allen, pharmacist

Left: *Nursing students and supervisor on a break from surgery socializing on the hospital roof, circa 1910-20.* Back of photograph identifies the group, left to right: *G. Ulstrup, H. Terrill, B. Powell, Mrs. Price, H. Burger, L. Vogel, Kim Yap, E. Barkley*

prompted Emma Wakeman to resign as hospital superintendent that same year, Loveridge assumed directorship of hospital operations and held that position until 1930. She tapped G.M. Welsh, a member of Good Samaritan's first graduating class, to succeed her as head of nursing. Bishop Morris himself died in 1906, mourned by what was reported to be the largest crowd ever attending a Portland memorial service to that point. Rev. Charles Scadding replaced Morris as board chairman.

Various personalities associated with the hospital in its early decades have remained part of its folklore. Andrew Spencer, an African American porter who had been sold as a slave in Tennessee, came to Oregon as a youth, and was relieved of blinding cataracts by surgeon Holt Wilson of the Good Samaritan staff. Spencer's years of dedicated service

earned him widely felt affection and loyalty. He was not above a bit of mischief with altruistic intent. By shorting together the bell wires that ran through his room, Spencer would call the nurses' attention to a crying baby that he judged to be in need of care. Another beloved figure, "Daddy Allen," served as the hospital's first professional pharmacist. Hired at the beginning of the century and continuing into the 1920s, Allen reportedly kept his compounds in unmarked containers, knowing them by sight, taste, or feel—and thereby perhaps enhancing his job security. Yet another well-known character, patient George Walter, entered Good Samaritan in 1923 with a gunshot wound that left him paralyzed from the waist down. Walter lived in the hospital for fifty-five years, assisted by a 1934 state legislative act providing him $100 a month. Despite over a dozen rounds of

Andrew Spencer, porter

Opposite: *1910, Surgery at Good Samaritan Hospital*

Carolyn Davis, hospital superintendent, 1930 to 1936

Opposite: *September 14, 1943, Army nurses taking oath of allegiance at Portland's Civic Auditorium.* Left to right: *Harriet McRay, Elizabeth Dement, Hazel Lintner, Ellen Dunn, Frances Gerdis, Hinewoa Seifert, Major B.P. Cody*

surgery, he remained unable to walk or stand. Bringing some entrepreneurial zeal to his situation, he added a special shelf to his wheelchair and sold "greeting cards, magazines, candy bars, cigarettes, and other items" to fellow patients and visitors. Unfortunately, he spent his last years in reclusion and depression.

After the United States entered World War I, 103 Good Samaritan nursing graduates served overseas, many of them at Base Hospital Forty-Six in France, near the Swiss border. A tireless Emily Loveridge corresponded faithfully with every former student performing such duty. Back at home, the influenza pandemic of 1918 overwhelmed Good Samaritan, like hospitals nationwide, with the scope of the domestic health crisis. Having already sent eleven nurses and two interns off to wartime service, the shorthanded hospital staff treated more than 1,200 patients in less than a year. The epidemic claimed 3,000 lives in Oregon, including four Good Samaritan nurses. An inquest following the epidemic attributed a relatively higher rate of flu death to Good Samaritan than to other hospitals and criticized the nursing staff for not wearing masks. In response, the trustees emphasized that Good Samaritan had remained open to all in need, whereas other institutions had restricted admission.

Whether treating flu sufferers, train wreck victims, or fire survivors, Loveridge kept patient care central to her professional code. By the time she retired in 1930, she oversaw a 300-bed hospital and followed "an inflexible rule" of visiting each patient daily. When she found it necessary to talk with any of several physicians who purported to be too busy to see her, she would purloin the offender's hat and return it only upon securing the desired conference. Her compassionate energy extended into her private life, for while living at the hospital, Loveridge raised her sister's two orphaned children as well as a third adopted child. Her public valedictory as chief administrator lay in seeing Good Samaritan earn "first-class ratings in all areas from the American College of Surgeons." Privately, she took comparable satisfaction in having reduced the working hours for student nurses, who, by the 1920s, put

in only forty-eight hours weekly at the hospital rather than the previously required seventy-two. In keeping with Loveridge's emphasis on theoretical and practical competence, however, the newer generation faced a more extensive and demanding curriculum to absorb their free time.

The 1930s saw considerable turnover in hospital leadership as Loveridge moved into retirement. Board chairman Bishop Walter Sumner (in office from 1915 to 1935) again turned to the school of nursing director and elevated Carolyn Davis to the post of hospital superintendent. Her six years of service coincided with the stringent economic realities dictated by the Great Depression. The sole building project of Davis's tenure was a residence hall for student nurses. Her eventual replacement, Dr. Charles Manlove, had previously established Portland's finest pathology laboratory at Good Samaritan. He had also introduced the city's first electrocardiograph machine. The decade literally ended with a bang on August 20, 1939, when convict-patient Robert Brumfield grabbed his guard's gun and attempted an escape. He shot and killed aide Hattie Hooker and wounded two others, including Manlove, whom he shot in the knee. The episode resulted in local police officers' thereafter wearing holsters with safety fasteners to secure their pistols from theft.

Manlove barely had a chance to recover from his knee injury before enlisting in the army at the outset of World War II. Alta Hollenbeck served as acting superintendent, though Manlove commuted back on weekends to Good Samaritan from his posting in Spokane. Under the direction of Good Samaritan physician A.G. Strohm, Base Hospital Forty-Six in France reopened. Performing more operations per day than in all Portland hospitals combined, Base Hospital Forty-Six consisted entirely of Oregonians: fifty doctors and one hundred nurses, among them a high percentage of Good Samaritan graduates. Unlike their World War I predecessors, however, they did not enjoy the privilege of correspondence with Emily Loveridge, who, on April 26, 1941, passed away at age eighty-one in the hospital she had served so faithfully since her arrival in 1890.

1960s, Center, Lloydena Grimes, director of nursing, 1952 to 1982, with students

A Hospital-Based Nursing Program Runs Its Course

So many nursing graduates and other clinical staff devoted themselves to the war that Good Samaritan relied heavily on volunteer labor until 1945. When the hospital's nurses returned from overseas at war's end to work in their single-sex profession, they found greater job security than women who had been doing other war-related work. Many women faculty members hired at Linfield College during the war, for example, were expected to resign when experienced male veterans once again became available as instructors.

The increasing demand for qualified nurses in the post-war years predictably swelled the size of classes at Good Samaritan. In the early 1950s the hospital became Portland's leading treatment center for victims of polio, an illness requiring intensive immediate treatment and extended therapy thereafter. Other institutional stresses surfaced during these years. In 1951, the nonmedical staff at the hospital staged a strike, setting up picket lines. Their demands for better wages and working conditions prompted eight months of negotiations, but the workers did not achieve the closed union shop they sought. The hospital's nurses and nursing faculty members did not participate in this labor action.

In 1952, direction of the School of Nursing passed into the hands of Lloydena Grimes, who held the position for the next three decades. During that time she contended with more changes in nursing education than in the preceding sixty years combined, though the transformation did not happen immediately. Throughout the 1950s and for most of the 1960s, student life continued to be defined by Loveridge's mode of whole-life commitment. When the hospital erected Loveridge Hall in 1966 to expand student housing, dorm regulations had barely changed from the days of its namesake. A publication celebrating transfer of the Good Samaritan nursing program to Linfield College in 1985 made clear that Lloydena Grimes had continued this austere code for roughly two decades:

> Restrictions were many, especially for the young probationary students. The student nurses were required to live in the dormitory and had to be in by 10 p.m. for the evening room check. One overnight pass was allowed per month. Students could not marry, and male visitors were confined to the first floor areas. Students stood up when an instructor or physician entered the room; it was completely unacceptable to question a physician's direction or make any kind of treatment-related decision.

But the impact of the 1960s made itself felt at Good Samaritan just as it had in McMinnville. While President Bjork dismantled in loco parentis regulations at Linfield College, Grimes came to recognize by the 1970s that student nurses now conducted and viewed themselves differently than in the past (see "'For the First Time . . .'" p. 105). She richly deserves credit not only for her professional longevity, but also for her constructive management and embrace of such change, particularly given its break from her own decades-long policies and personal code of professionalism. At her retirement in 1982, the Good Samaritan trustees honored her leadership by establishing the Lloydena Grimes Nursing Scholarship Fund.

In this period the contemporary nursing curriculum underwent as much transformation as student life did. An explosion in the use of technology, combined with increasing medical specialization, demanded no less. Recognizing the underlying pathology of disease and developing the ability to interpret information from sophisticated diagnostic instruments became increasingly central to nursing practice.

This provoked a paradigm shift as nursing education gravitated toward the physicians' medical model even while retaining its traditional care emphasis. To support this curricular realignment, Grimes secured approval in 1968 for a modern Nursing Education Building (now Peterson Hall) to place conventional lecture and office spaces alongside the laboratories increasingly demanded by the discipline. With married persons no longer excluded from the profession, recruitment of more mature students meant that many more women (and the occasional man) came seeking a second career or planning to enter the workplace for the first time after having raised a family. Predictably, this new clientele lacked the deferential tendencies of their traditional-aged predecessors, further changing the climate of contemporary nursing education.

Ironically, the same movement toward greater professionalism that transformed Good Samaritan School of Nursing in the 1970s led to its demise as a freestanding institution in the 1980s. Adopting components of the medical model greatly strained the school's three-year curriculum. Demand for more basic knowledge in such fields as pathology and pharmacology went hand in hand with more specialized nursing practice. By 1975 Good Samaritan found itself the only hospital-based diploma nursing program in the state. Increasingly, nursing education became the precinct of accredited two- and four-year programs at institutions of higher education that required a full complement of science, humanities, and social science courses before specialized nursing study could begin. Demand grew for academically prepared nursing faculty who held advanced degrees and conducted basic research. Good Samaritan's commitment to research expanded steadily throughout the 1950s and beyond. Among the hospital's various laboratories, one in neurophysiology headed by Linfield College trustee Olof Larsell helped set the stage for the college's later acquisition of the nursing program (see "Trustee and Teacher," p. 106).

By the time Lloydena Grimes retired in 1982, it fell to her successor, Patricia Hough, to negotiate the end of diploma

Connecting Life
"For the First Time..."

The early 1970s brought tumultuous change to the Good Samaritan School of Nursing just as it did to Linfield College. Sharry Fasset, student body president at the nursing school for 1970-71, summed up the year as follows:

For the class of '71 change was an every day event. Students who entered GSH with dreams of becoming a sensitive bedside nurse were suddenly confronted with an explosion of medical technology and insensitive machines to care for in addition to their patients. Even our roles as women were being jolted by the "Women's Liberation Movement."

For the first time at GSH students were not confined to their rooms for "study hours" each evening.

For the first time students could marry and remain in the program.

For the first time a male student was accepted into the nursing program.

For the first time a student could wear brown nylon stockings on duty.

The first course in "Human Sexuality" was given to the students.

For the first time nurses were allowed to remain seated in the presence of a physician.

For the first time it became acceptable in certain situations (ICU and Isolation) to remove your nurse's cap while on duty.

For the first time a few doctors and nurses addressed each other by first names.

Connecting Learning
Trustee and Teacher

Immediately following graduation from McMinnville College in 1910, Olof Larsell joined the faculty, teaching science for three years. He proceeded to Northwestern University to earn a PhD in anatomy prior to his appointment to the faculty at the University of Oregon Medical School, where he spent the remainder of his career. After joining Linfield's Board of Trustees in 1922, he served for forty-two years and was the only academic ever to hold the board chairmanship (1931 to 1938).

Olof's son Frank, also a Linfield graduate, died in combat during World War II. Family and friends subsequently established the Frank S. Larsell Memorial Lectureship at the college, with Olof Larsell delivering the series lecture in 1951. His contribution, "Tadpoles and Brains," drew upon his research in neuroscience. That work culminated in a posthumously published textbook, *The Comparative Anatomy and Histology of the Cerebellum* (1967), introduced by Larsell's longtime colleague Robert S. Dow. Another Linfield alumnus (class of 1929), Dow also distinguished himself as a neuroscientist.

Larsell's scholarship demonstrates the breadth one might expect of a liberal arts graduate. He wrote on the practice of medicine during the Lewis and Clark expedition before many others had approached the topic and in 1947 published *The Doctor in Oregon*, the definitive history of medical practice in the territory and state. Much of what we know about the early years of the Good Samaritan Hospital, where Larsell conducted the bulk of his research, derives from this volume. He earned many academic distinctions including appointment as a Fulbright Scholar to Sweden in 1955.

In 1962, Larsell and Dow launched a joint Linfield–Good Samaritan Hospital master of science program in neurophysiology. Though the 1962-64 Linfield catalog advertised the degree, Larsell's death put a quick end to the program. Nonetheless, the esteem felt for Olof Larsell at both Good Samaritan and Linfield, along with the continuing presence of Dow at the hospital, paved the way for the nursing affiliation agreement that would link the two institutions in 1982.

1912, Olof Larsell as a Linfield faculty member

education at Good Samaritan Hospital. Increasing specialization had already required Good Samaritan to seek clinical placements for students beyond the walls of their single hospital. The fierce competition from opposite ends of the educational spectrum posed even greater challenges. On one hand, prospective students could pay significantly less and have a more flexible life by studying at a community college, which still qualified them to sit for the examination to become a registered nurse. The ample numbers of community college graduates filled slots for entry-level nursing jobs based predominantly on the care model. While Good Samaritan graduates could successfully compete with such candidates, the market for lower-paying jobs was flooded. At the other end of the spectrum, higher-paying positions began going to candidates holding bachelor's degrees, which a national accreditation movement touted as essential to more specialized nursing practice. Predictably, this movement heavily favored programs affiliated with a college or university. Baccalaureate programs at Oregon Health & Science University and the University of Portland became more and more attractive to ambitious applicants who had once aspired to Good Samaritan. The challenge of meeting national accreditation standards made it clear that the hospital should either close its program or seek affiliation with a four-year collegiate partner.

When Good Samaritan's trustees acted on this dilemma by inviting merger proposals from interested institutions, Linfield College stood at a strategic crossroads of its own. President Charles Walker had already concluded that a Portland-area presence would enhance the college's regional reputation and visibility. Equally important, Linfield's Dr. John Day had already successfully launched an experimental bachelor of arts program in liberal studies for Good Samaritan's diploma graduates.

Even with such auguries in Linfield's favor, a successful affiliation agreement took considerable time to gestate. During the 1980-82 negotiation period, the market for nurses soured relative to both earlier and later periods. Though a

diploma-based nursing program had outlived its historical moment, the state's capacity to support another full bachelor's program remained uncertain. The novelty of a merger between two of Oregon's oldest educational entities (*the* oldest in Good Samaritan's case) held both attractions and risks. A thirty-eight-mile physical separation reinforced significant cultural differences between the two institutions. Whereas Linfield's ethos of inspired pragmatism had led it to develop other professional programs such as business, journalism, and education, each of these had grown up organically within the faculty itself. The leaders of every such effort had had to negotiate, from day one, what it meant to function as a professional program within a liberal arts context. The pro-

posed Linfield–Good Samaritan merger represented something entirely different–absorption of an autonomous professional program with little or no prior grounding in the liberal arts. Faculty members on both sides expressed reservations. In McMinnville, concern arose over lack of doctorally prepared nursing faculty. At Good Samaritan, faculty members worried that their program's hallmark grounding in hands-on clinical training would succumb before an academically driven curricular focus.

Financial risks also weighed heavily on the various decision makers. Given the risks of merger and the need to build enrollment in a tight market for nursing students, negotiations stalled over the apportioning of revenues and risks.

Left: *1977, Dr. John Day with second graduate cohort from the Good Samaritan BA degree completion program, forerunner of Linfield's Division of Continuing Education*

Good Samaritan trustees rejected an initial proposal that both institutions share equally in revenues and responsibility for potential losses. Linfield then proposed to assume all risk of financial loss in exchange for all revenues (after payment of fixed costs borne by Good Samaritan and stipulated in the agreement). This proposal was accepted, clearing the way for Linfield College to exercise full administrative and curricular control over nursing education at the new Linfield–Good Samaritan School of Nursing. The agreement signed in 1982 stipulated a three-year transitional period so that the final class of diploma students could graduate under Good Samaritan auspices.

On June 8, 1985, an event entitled "Celebrating Ninety-Five Years of Excellence in Nursing Education" occurred in Portland to mark the end of the road for the Good Samaritan Hospital School of Nursing. Emily Loveridge had placed the beaver on its logo and nursing pin as a symbol of the school, chosen, she said, because it was "an animal of industry . . . and on the first seal of Oregon." At the 1985 ceremony, called a "bittersweet occasion" by Governor Victor Atiyeh, the lamp Loveridge had cherished as a symbol of nursing adopted by her beloved Florence Nightingale passed from Good Samaritan to Linfield College. Simultaneously, a new nursing pin came into being, the beaver replaced by an open book, one of two traditional Linfield symbols (the other being the Old Oak). This new pin highlighted the integration of nursing education with Linfield's liberal arts emphasis on intellectual inquiry. From this point onward the parallel story of the Good Samaritan Nursing School became part of the unfolding story that is Linfield College. ∎

Left: 2007, *Loveridge Hall on the Portland Campus*

Opposite: 2007, *Students at Linfield's Portland campus in the class entitled Life Threatening Health Challenges access the vital signs of a computerized "simulated person."* Left to right: *Jenna Bowker, Christina Breen, and Laurel Anderson*

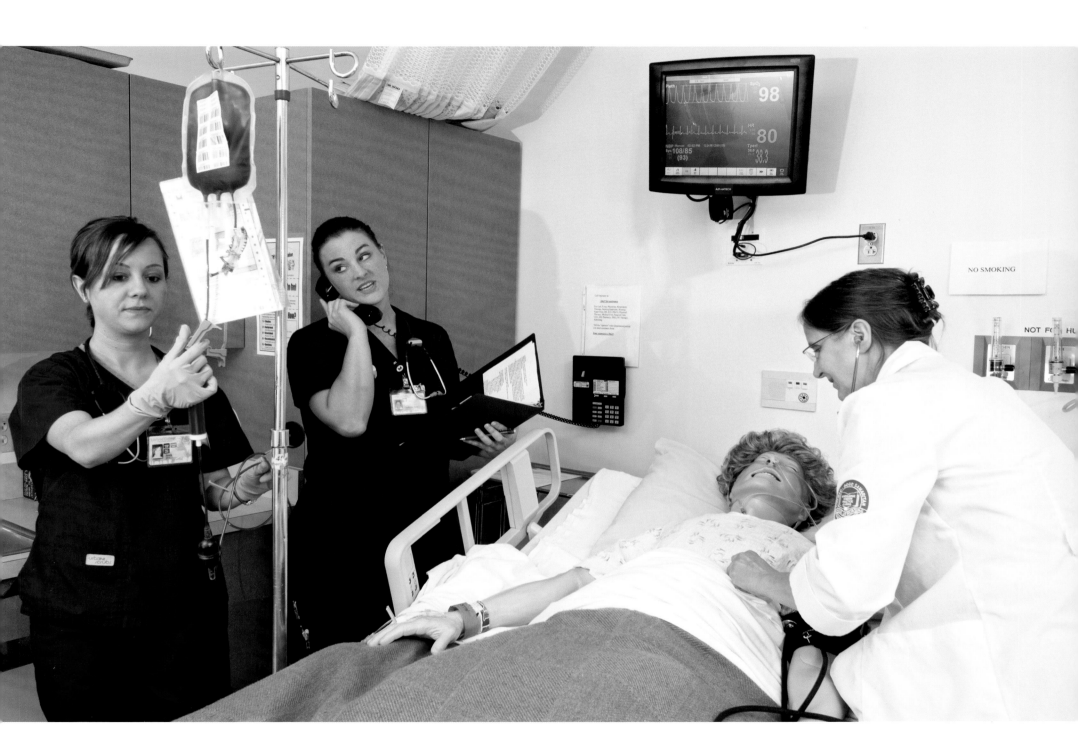

The Unfolding Story

At an annual campus gathering on March 5, 1970, trustee chairman Philip Renshaw told his fellow alumni: "I would guess that Linfield's chances of surviving its thirteenth decade as a viable private college are about fifty-fifty." He had said the same thing privately to the trustees, seeking to motivate them to shake off the casual oversight to which they had grown accustomed during the Dillin era. Four years later, with the economy worsening and confidence in President Bjork waning, Linfield stood in even weaker financial shape. Yet in other key respects the college had become stronger by 1974. Its academic reputation had improved, public programming had expanded to include a lineup of stimulating outside speakers, students now enjoyed the campus freedoms a new generation presumed as its right, and the administrative structure emulated a shared governance model touted by many elite private colleges. Even the turmoil among trustees and around the president harbored a potential positive side. Worn down by conflict, the various college constituencies collectively hungered for effective new leadership.

Two preliminary steps prepared the institution for that change. First, Dr. Winthrop Dolan accepted an invitation to serve as acting president for a second time from June through August of 1974. Dolan had opposed the faculty's motion of no confidence in President Bjork and had protested the means used to bring it before the Faculty Assembly. But even those who disagreed with him knew that his actions rested on principle, that he took disinterested positions, and that he understood how to heal institutional wounds. As Dolan returned to the classroom for the fall semester, the second acting president arrived in the person of Cornelius Siemens, recent director of international programs for the California state university system. Siemens was still in England when Harry Dillin recommended him to the Linfield board, having gotten to know him years earlier during Siemens's presidencies at Compton College (1946-1960) and Humboldt State University (1960-1973). A Baptist, Siemens also satisfied the requirement that Linfield's president hold that religious affiliation—a stricture the trustees eliminated from the bylaws before they launched their search for a permanent president. They did so to increase their applicant pool amidst the turmoil facing private higher education nationally, with some colleges closing for good, dozens of others struggling, and the pressures around college presidencies escalating due to the student rights movement.

Reassembling the Pieces

For a while the solution to Linfield's leadership challenges seemed to lie outside academia. Private contacts suggested that second-term Governor Tom McCall might consider the position, and so the search committee and Executive Committee of the board voted unanimously on September 7, 1974,

Opposite: *2007, Jereld R. Nicholson Library*

111

to offer him the presidency. Unlike the private offer to Governor Mark Hatfield in 1966, Linfield's courting of McCall became a public affair. He visited the campus on several occasions and at times appeared about to accept. Though Portland newspapers speculated on a positive outcome, in January 1975 the governor declined the offer, consenting instead to election as a trustee.

Meanwhile college leaders had continued to assess other applicants, and in March the Executive Committee recommended Dr. Charles U. Walker for the Linfield presidency. The full board ratified this motion on May 31, 1975. Walker proved exceptionally well suited to lead the institution at a crossroads moment almost as dire as that faced by Leonard Riley in 1906. Having earned his Stanford University PhD in education by studying that institution's organizational management, he came to Linfield fresh from the presidency of Russell Sage College in New York. In his first interview in *The Linfield College Bulletin*, he wryly told of an "unsuccessful attempt [in 1964] to get a teaching position at a small college in the Pacific Northwest, named Linfield." Over the next seventeen years, Walker not only turned the college around but set it on a steady upward trajectory both academically and financially.

Luckily Walker, unlike Riley, did not find the cupboard entirely bare on his arrival. The Linfield Plan worked better than its detractors had predicted, increasing enrollment above projections in both the new winter and summer blocks. Acting President Siemens balanced the operating budget for the first time since 1966-67, aided by the combined impact of the institution-wide 5-percent salary cut imposed by Bjork's last budget, additional enrollment revenues, and a reinvigorated McMinnville campaign that raised $65,000. That effort, co-led by Harry Dillin and local trustee Eugene Marsh, assumed the title "Partners in Progress." Joint community and college leadership over the ensuing three decades has made the yearly fund-raising effort a nationally recognized exemplar of productive town-gown relations.

Still, from the vantage of 1975, Linfield's survival remained precarious. When asked by the trustees about formal inauguration plans, Walker concluded that any such celebration should wait until "the accumulated deficit is eradicated." Installed without fanfare, he rolled up his sleeves and set to work. At his opening convocation address in September, he proclaimed: "Hold your head up high, put a smile on your face and a spring in your step. Together we are starting a new year." President Walker thus defined his tenure by an unrelenting optimism about the prospects of the institution he had come to serve. Drawing on precepts from his own educational background as well as the college's traditional blend of inspirational fervor and practicality, Walker quite literally enacted pragmatic philosopher William James's thesis (in the essay "The Will to Believe") that confidence in one's prospects actually fosters success. Linfield stood poised to renew a mission that had long melded high spiritual and educational aims with common sense.

In keeping with his expertise in higher education organizational design, Walker soon adjusted the college's practices to improve effectiveness at all levels. In short order he ensured that trustees and administrators alike regularly established goals and reported on their progress. His creativity in managing unexpected problems also surfaced early on. By late summer 1976, for example, freshman enrollment had grown 21 percent over the previous fall, but years of budget cutbacks meant that staffing and maintenance of the residence halls proved unequal to this good fortune. In a representative initiative, Walker launched "Operation Pitch-In," whereby he and his wife, Cherie, led more than 100 volunteer staffers and community members to prepare rooms for the new student arrivals. Certainly the extra hands proved crucial to the project's goals, but its real genius lay in creating a shared sense of purpose within and beyond the campus. Over these early years the president and his new dean of academic affairs, John Housley (see "Three Exemplary Deans," p. 114), presided at countless potluck dinners,

Opposite: *1982, President Charles Walker and students*

(see "Three Exemplary Deans," p. 114)

Win Dolan   *Colena Anderson*   *Jack Housley*

Connecting Learning
Three Exemplary Deans

In addition to Emanuel Northup, Carrie Potter, William R. Frerichs, and Steine Jonasson—each celebrated in other vignettes—three distinguished college administrators, Winthrop "Win" Dolan, Colena Anderson, and John P. "Jack" Housley, deserve special notice.

Win Dolan, an alumnus of Denison University and the holder of a PhD from the University of Oklahoma, came to Linfield in 1941 as professor of mathematics and dean of academic administration. He had already served a stint as dean and acting president of Bacone College, an American Indian school in Oklahoma. He performed key calculations for Walter Dyke and Kenneth Trolan at the Linfield Research Institute and coauthored many of their early publications. Though he contemplated moving to Femcor Corporation at its founding, he concluded that his heart lay more in teaching than in research. Several times he retired as dean, but when his various replacements did not work out, merit and a fair-minded temper kept returning him to administration until his last such service under President Gordon Bjork in 1968. He twice served Linfield as acting president.

Dolan also taught astronomy and, one year after retiring, published *A Choice of Sundials* (1975). His interest in measuring time without mechanics is commemorated in the stainless steel and copper sundial (designed by professor of art Nils Lou) on the south side of Murdock Hall. Dolan served as a college trustee from 1974 until 1989.

Colena Anderson, a 1914 graduate in English from Cornell University, returned to McMinnville from Redlands, California, soon after the 1944 death of her husband (and former Linfield president), Dr. Elam Anderson. Invited to do so, she arrived back at Linfield in 1946 to teach history and English. In 1953-54 she took a leave at age 63 to complete her doctorate in Far East Studies from Claremont. She also served two terms as Linfield's dean of women.

Colena Anderson's friendship in China with Nobel Prize–winning author Pearl S. Buck piqued Anderson's interest in creative writing. Before and after retirement in 1954, she published stories, poems, articles, and several books, including *Handbook for Christian Writers* and *Joy Beyond Grief*. She insisted the latter, a guide to widowhood, should have been entitled *Renewal Beyond Grief* despite publishers' objections.

Jack Housley became dean of faculty in 1976. A native of the U.S. Southwest and a graduate from the University of New Mexico, Housley received his PhD from Union Theological Seminary in 1961, writing his dissertation on Christian theology in Latin America. Unlike most other notable senior administrators at the college, Housley was not blessed with longevity: he died at age fifty-one during only his seventh year in office.

In that short time, Housley earned as much affection and respect among his colleagues as anyone ever to lead the faculty. A special memorial passed by the Faculty Assembly lauded his "critical and perceptive leadership in such areas as International and Honors programs, faculty development, and the college's lecture series." President Charles Walker celebrated Housley as "a cosmopolitan, at ease with all kinds of people, who never felt a need to put on airs to be anything other than what he truly was."

targeting all Linfield constituencies and enlisting the assistance of each in planning for the future. The *Linfield Bulletin* assiduously communicated good news about the activities of faculty, students, and alumni. Issue after upbeat issue offered evidence of a community recovering its common purpose and knitting itself back together.

Arriving as the college's first non-Baptist president, Walker also faced the challenge of redefining the place of faith in the college's institutional saga. Some in the surrounding community had unfairly charged Bjork with overseeing a slide into unbelief. Countering that impression, Walker began a fund-raising campaign to establish a full-time chaplain as a means of reaching out to the American Baptist churches. Simultaneously, he led the trustees to adopt "A Religious Commitment" in 1976 to outline a broad, ecumenical perspective on religious affairs at the college. Walter Dyke and Hugh Dowd, once again celebrated at the college for their prior accomplishments, returned as overt supporters of Linfield. The debates of previous decades over the college's spiritual mission ceased in some cases and in others fell dormant as college leaders deliberately sought to restore institutional stability.

Linfield's academic resurgence rested on four major initiatives: systematic emphasis on international study, a new program of faculty development, successful expansion into adult education, and absorption of the Good Samaritan diploma nursing program. Each of these initiatives fostered hope that days of retrenchment and shared sacrifice would soon end.

Although global awareness had functioned as an institutional value since Elam Anderson's presidency, efforts at international study had lacked a coherent and purposeful educational focus in the intervening decades, having rested primarily on missionary work or an individual faculty member's selective interest. Under Walker's leadership the faculty devised a more comprehensive approach that took advantage of international course options within the block system. For the first time the college negotiated a formal standing

relationship with an overseas partner: on July 29, 1976, Linfield signed a sister college agreement with Kanto Gakuin University in Yokohama, Japan. Major grants followed the Kanto Gakuin initiative to support Linfield faculty in studying foreign languages and cultures. Dean Housley launched a diversified faculty development program that was psychologically bolstering even if financially modest. Thus began a steadily expanding commitment to global studies so central to Linfield's contemporary self-definition that the college now boasts a high percentage of faculty and senior administrators with international experience.

The foray into adult education led by John Day had been inspired by his visiting a successful program of the sort at the University of Redlands and believing it well suited to the ethos of Linfield. Day thus became the inaugural director of what would grow into the Division of Continuing Education, though he left this position before long to head alumni relations. The DCE program targeted adults in the workforce who had not yet begun or had not completed undergraduate degrees. Volunteer Linfield faculty members undertook overload teaching for this program (in classes conducted in the evenings and on weekends) partly because of the understandable desire for supplemental income, but also because of the opportunity to extend to adult learners Linfield's passion for "making winners, not selecting them." Through their efforts in the 1970s and 1980s, the college developed the largest and most flexible program of adult education in the state of Oregon. When other institutions began zealously targeting so-called "non-

Left: *1983, International students*

*1982, Linfield President Charles Walker and Good Samaritan CEO
Chester Stocks at the affiliation agreement signing*

1988, Dean Pamela Harris, third from left, *celebrating National League of
Nursing accreditation with students,* left to right: *Ellen Bernhard, Trent
Morgan, Joyce Thody, Cindy Houghton, and Mary Frymire*

traditional students" in the 1990s, Linfield's adult program yielded its status as the state's largest such venture, but it remains academically strong and well respected.

As described in chapter three, Linfield's entry into nursing education took two main routes. One followed Olof Larsell's attempt at a cooperative program for granting a master's degree in neurophysiology. The second involved John Day's liberal arts program for nurses, which awarded BA degrees to the college's first cohort of thirteen adult learners in May 1976. Thanks to these prior affiliations, when the Good Samaritan School of Nursing sought a four-year college partner to launch a bachelor of science in nursing degree in 1980, Linfield held a distinct edge over other colleges bidding for the opportunity. Negotiations concluded in 1982 with the signing of a legal agreement between the boards of Linfield College and Good Samaritan Hospital and Medical Center. The Linfield-Good Samaritan School of Nursing then readied itself to accept applicants for the projected BSN degree. For three years the new program operated alongside the existing one; the freestanding Good Samaritan School of Nursing graduated its last class in 1985.

Some elements of the transition proved rockier than anticipated. The Linfield dean of nursing, Dr. Paul Gaspodarski, left prematurely. His successor, Dr. Pamela Harris, arrived in 1984 and set the college's sights on securing accreditation by the National League of Nursing, a status not required to award the new BSN degree but vital to the school's future credibility. Also at this time, a new dean of faculty, Dr. Kenneth Goodrich, capably filled the shoes of Dean Housley, whose death in 1983 after a long illness had left the campus community reeling. Though the first application for accreditation was denied, Deans Goodrich and Harris led the nursing faculty in the sustained efforts that finally secured full National League of Nursing accreditation in 1988. Throughout the transition, both programs remained fully accredited by the Oregon League of Nursing, which controlled the right of graduates to sit for the registered nurse examination. In 1989 Good Samaritan Hospital ceased independent operation, merging with HealthLink, owner of four other Portland-area hospitals, under the name Legacy Health Systems. It is this organization that today partners with Linfield in nursing education.

Even before Walker retired the previously accumulated debt (a feat accomplished in 1981), the trustees showed their

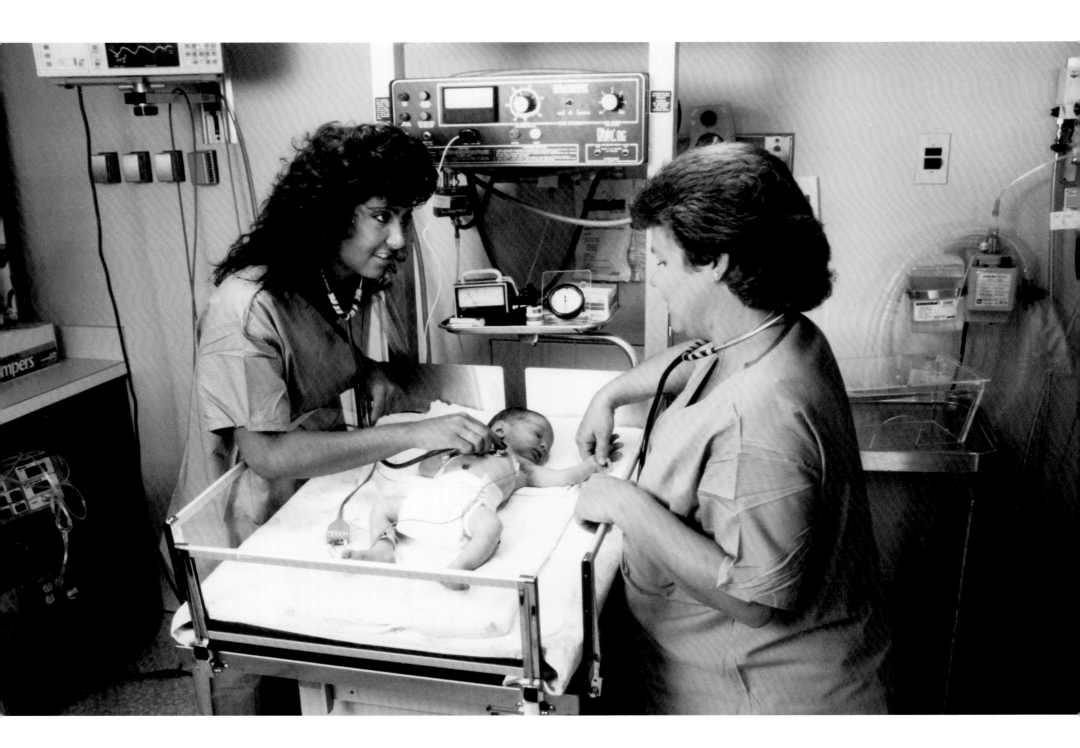

1973, Pi Kappa Alpha Fraternity.
Left to right, front to back: *Scott Wells, Greg Jenney, Dixon Rauch, Alden Richards, Steve Weidmann, Tim Stephenson, Mark Erickson, Robert Stephenson, Dan Belderrain, Dick Weber, Bill Bailey, Doug McBride, Gary Munson, Eric Wells, Greg Minckley, Rick Morrill, Walter Kruse, Steve Hagan, Bob Crump, Mike Mitchell, Eric Neste, Gary Hill, Dan Waritz, Bill Wallace, Randy Celle, Greg Cody, Jim Franklin, Ed Edinger*

pocketbook beyond repair." This combination of attributes was nothing new: Linfield had long provided access for students of modest means.

Walker orchestrated a number of other high-profile firsts for Linfield. In 1981, the college secured several major grants to establish itself as one of only five institutions worldwide permitted by Sweden's Nobel Foundation to use its name for a permanent lectureship. To this day the Oregon Nobel Laureate Symposium brings Nobel Prize winners to campus for public lectures, panels, and classroom visits. Similarly, in a 1979 report by the National Academy of Sciences, the college again earned praise for continuing its stellar track record of graduating future science PhDs. This recognition underscored the fund-raising campaign's focus on a new science building to house the departments of biology and chemistry. In another testament to the campaign's success, Murdock Hall opened in 1982. And in the arts, a new creative writing program housed within the English department was among the first of its kind at the baccalaureate level in the Northwest.

The activist fervor among students of the late 1960s and early 1970s faded at Linfield as at other colleges, but it did not disappear entirely. In 1985, the students declared campus a "nuclear-free zone," and shortly thereafter petitioned the trustees to divest endowment holdings in companies doing business in apartheid-ridden South Africa. But the political rhetoric had changed from the previous decade. Rather than presenting their position as a demand, students and faculty advocating for divestiture effectively encouraged the board to consider alternative investment strategies, which the trustees in their turn vetted against their fiduciary responsibilities. In 1988, having satisfied themselves on the latter point, they adopted a policy to divest the college portfolio of South African holdings.

Notable successes in intercollegiate athletics assisted Linfield's march into the limelight. The women's basketball program won three consecutive conference championships from 1978 through 1980. The men's track team took conference honors in 1980, recovering for one season a trophy that

confidence in him by endorsing an $18-million comprehensive fund-raising campaign entitled Vision for the Future. President Bjork had been correct to insist that a favorable academic reputation held the key to the college's ongoing stability, but sustaining and enhancing that profile required increased reliable income. Walker's organizational genius and persistence in cultivating donors allowed the campaign, launched in 1981, to exceed its goal by $2 million. The campaign drew welcome momentum from Linfield's recognition in regional and national media, visibility that peaked with *Money* magazine's November 1979 identification of Linfield as one of the top ten private colleges in the nation to "offer a quality education without crunching the family

Connecting Community
Heard on Campus

A tale of Linfield's rising prominence from the 1980s to the present day may be told in the national and international profile of its campus visitors. Some examples, clockwise from bottom left: 1981, former Secretary of State Henry Kissinger with Cherie Walker; 1988, former President Gerald Ford with the Walkers; 1988, former President Jimmy Carter autographs a book for Linfield's Dr. Peter Richardson and Beverly Richardson; 1988, Nobel Peace Prize winner, author, and Holocaust survivor Elie Wiesel; 1968, former Vice President Richard

Nixon on the presidential campaign trail with Professor Roy D. Mahaffey, whose debate tournament Nixon attended on the Linfield campus while he was a student at Whittier College, California, in the early 1930s; 1994, Anita Hill on the lecture circuit following her sexual harassment allegations against Clarence Thomas during his U.S. Senate confirmation hearing to become associate justice of the Supreme Court; (center) 1981, Metropolitan Opera singer Beverly Sills at a lecture on her life as an artist.

1961, Coach Paul Durham and his Wildcats were all smiles after defeating Whittier College, 18-7, in the first post-season football game in Linfield history. The victory propelled the Wildcats into the NAIA Camellia Bowl championship against Pittsburg State, which capitalized on a key Linfield turnover to win 12-7.

Connecting Life
The Streak

In September 1956, a football team playing for a college with an undistinguished lifetime record (102-146-20) began its season by tying 0-0 with Portland State University. No Linfield head coach with at least two seasons at the helm sported a record with more wins than losses and ties. Even the storied Henry Lever had gone 30-54-7 over twelve seasons, and incumbent coach Paul Durham's record amounted to 32-35-4 over eight seasons.

So much for past performance as prologue. The 1956 Linfield football team ended its season with a record of 6-1-2 and won the conference championship. Paul Durham went on in his final twelve seasons to earn a winning record of 90-16-6 and seven conference championships. His successor, Ad Rutschman (see "Coaching as Teaching," p. 126), won an astounding fifteen conference championships in twenty-four years of coaching.

During Rutschman's era, Linfield gained steadily on Notre Dame University and Harvard University—tied for the most consecutive winning seasons, at any level of competition, in collegiate football history. Dubbed "The Streak," this record passed into Linfield's hands in 1993 when the college claimed its forty-third consecutive winning season under head coach Ed Langsdorf.

The Streak continues through the 2006 season, the last before this volume's publication. Jay Locey, head coach from 1998 to 2005, extended The Streak to fifty consecutive seasons in his final year. Responsibility for holding onto The Streak now falls on Joe Smith, who extended it with a winning season in his first year.

During its now fifty-one years of consecutive winning seasons, the Linfield football program boasts an imposing record of 497-240-30. It has garnered four national championships, going undefeated in each of those seasons. Anyone who thinks The Streak's continuation inevitable must avoid hubris, however, by pondering the history of football at Linfield before that auspicious season of 1956.

2004, Wildcats Quarterback Brett Elliot, all-time NCAA leader (all levels) in touchdown passes in a single season (61), throws against Occidental College in a playoff game en route to the NCAA Division III championship.

had been held exclusively by Linfield from 1973 to 1976. Under Coach Ad Rutschman, who also served as athletic director, football teams in 1982, 1984, and 1986 won national NAIA championships. The women's volleyball team placed second nationally in 1981, the highest placement by a Linfield women's team until Coach Jackson Vaughan led the 2007 softball team to the National Collegiate Athletic Association (NCAA) Division III title—the college's first-ever national women's championship.

With hardly a pause, Walker and the trustees launched a second major fund-raising campaign, The Linfield Advance-

ment Plan, in 1986. Its ambitious $34-million goal included $14 million for a new athletics complex and comprehensive remodeling of the Riley Student Center. Rebuilding the badly depleted endowment ranked high among the campaign's goals. It topped $38.5 million in 1992, the year following Walker's retirement announcement. To heighten the college's profile during this campaign, Walker earmarked endowment earnings created or bolstered during his presidency to secure speakers of national and international renown. This effort hit its peak in 1988, when former President Gerald Ford delivered the inaugural Edith Green Distinguished Lectureship,

Left: 1982, Linfield's football team celebrates its first national championship.

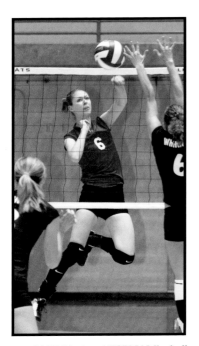

2005, National ESPN Volleyball Academic All-American of the Year Lindsay Harksen executes a kill.

1993, Rhea Heartleib playing lacrosse for the Wildcats

former President Jimmy Carter spoke on campus as the Pollard Symposium's Frazee Lecturer, and renowned Holocaust writer and human rights activist Elie Wiesel keynoted the Nobel Laureate Symposium.

The seventeen-year Walker presidency had produced much to celebrate as it drew to a close. Each year the college had operated within a balanced budget, usually finding itself in surplus. While McMinnville remained its home base, the nursing school and Division of Continuing Education had extended the college's reach to Portland and eight other centers in Oregon and Washington. Overseas opportunities now enabled half of Linfield graduates to study abroad at some point during their undergraduate careers. Sciences and athletics, two foci of Linfield excellence, occupied new facilities. The trustees recognized these achievements by naming the newly remodeled (now freestanding) portion of the old student center "Walker Hall." Standing across a new courtyard from Riley Student Center, Walker Hall linked its namesake's legacy for all time to that of the earlier "rescue president."

A New Kind of Pioneer

In concert with its frontier heritage, Linfield had always been coeducational and had hired women faculty members from its earliest days. Yet its leadership had remained predominantly male, in keeping with the times. The surface appearance of gender equality within the faculty also weakens upon closer inspection. Jane-Claire Dirks Edmunds, the first woman graduate later to earn a PhD and return to her alma mater, joined the college staff as an assistant in the registrar's office and only acquired teaching duties as an afterthought. Colena Anderson (see "Three Exemplary Deans," p. 112), widow of President Elam Anderson, eventually went on to earn her own PhD, serve as dean of women, and teach history for many years, but her rise within the college infrastructure derived from her earlier history as president's wife. Among the trustees, Mrs. Linfield remained a singular female presence on the board in having been invited to join on the basis of her business acumen. Other

women of prominence in the institutional record served due to their status as widows of former trustees (Jane Failing) or as nominees from Baptist constituencies who exercised little personal influence on decisions. Within the student body, the first two women presidents of the Associated Students, Gladys Strong in 1917, and Jocelle Fulham in 1943, secured election during periods of war when male enrollment dipped dramatically.

In these ways Linfield's limited inclusion of women in the institution's power centers mirrored the larger society. Pressed by Linfield trustee and Congresswoman Edith Green (whose own career shaped gender politics nationally, given her coauthorship of federal Title IX legislation in 1972), Linfield expanded the ranks of women faculty through fair and open hiring practices. Walker's presidency also oversaw the installation of a salary step system for faculty, motivated in part by an institutional commitment to redressing gender inequity in previous compensation practices. As the numbers of women students grew during the 1970s and 1980s—particularly at liberal arts colleges—their participation in disciplines beyond those traditionally sanctioned for women (teaching, home economics, nursing) expanded accordingly, with the paradoxical consequence that Linfield's Department of Consumer and Family Studies (heir to home economics) suffered such severe enrollment decline that it was officially dismantled. And while women athletes at the college found numerous opportunities to compete at the intercollegiate level, debate over Title IX's implications for gender ratios in athletics surfaced at the end of Walker's tenure and provoked a major struggle during the early presidency of his successor.

After an intensive national search, the board invited Dr. Vivian A. Bull to lead the college, impressed by her background in international education, experience in business, and full professorship in Drew University's department of economics. Upon arriving at Linfield in fall 1992, President Bull moved the college firmly into the Internet age. At the time, Linfield had little infrastructure to support computer-aided instruction or assist faculty to access online information and

Connecting Life
Dyke's Pragmatic Legacy

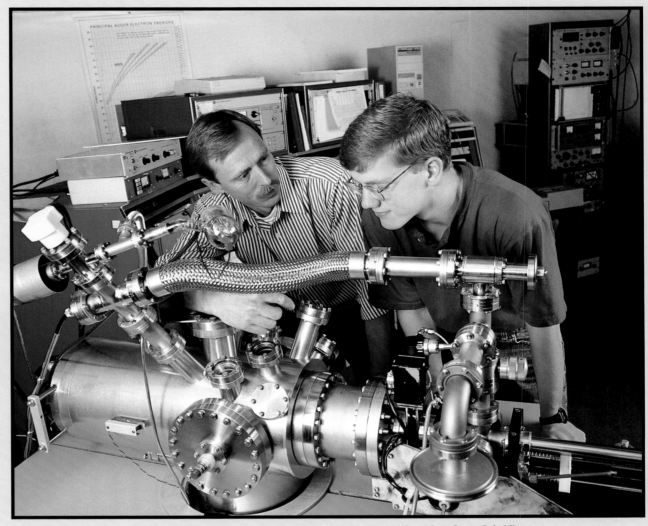

1997, Professor of Physics Bill Mackie works at a scanning Auger microscope with student Scott C. Williams.

The senior Walter Dyke graduated from McMinnville College in 1904. His skills in forensics prepared him well for his later career as a prominent Forest Grove attorney. After graduation, he maintained close ties with President Riley and watched with approval as his classmates from both the collegiate and secondary courses electrified the campus—literally—in 1907. Wiring installed entirely by student labor served the college until Harry Dillin decided to replace it in 1947.

Dyke senior became a trustee in 1914 and served until his early death in 1934. In the same year his son, Walter P. Dyke, enrolled to study physics under Professor Herschel Hewitt. The younger Dyke knew, both from family heritage and from Hewitt, that Linfield students seldom worked on science apparatus purchased outright. Instead, they built what they needed from scratch, plugging their self-designed instruments into electrical sockets wired by their apprentice predecessors.

The narrative of *The Untold Story* recounts the junior Dyke's founding of the Linfield Research Institute and Femcor. It likewise deals with his tempestuous career as he followed his father onto the Board of Trustees. For all his defects in diplomacy, Walter P. Dyke's life story reflects the highest ideals of the college in promoting "both theoretical and practical knowledge." At his death in 1995, his name appeared on forty-three peer-reviewed journal articles, and he held stake in thirty-three patents. He and his colleagues not only discovered new underlying principles in field emission theory, but also built by hand the apparatus detailed schematically in their patent applications.

While Dyke's financial legacy lives on directly in his many gifts to Linfield, much of the contemporary character of the college also reflects his influence. The doubling of campus acreage in 1999 resulted from the history linking Dyke's Linfield career to the Hewlett-Packard Corporation (see p. 131). The Murdock Charitable Trust, of which Dyke had been a founding trustee, not only provided major support for a new science building but also awarded Linfield a lecture-and-collaborative-research endowment graced with Dyke's name. Perhaps his strongest legacy lies in the many opportunities he created at Linfield for research in the sciences. His example and the opportunities provided by the Linfield Research Institute have inspired other notable spin-offs into applied physics by faculty and students.

Dyke's Femcor and LRI colleagues Lynwood Swanson (also a former Linfield dean of faculty) and Noel Martin (an alumnus and Linfield physics instructor), along with Lloyd Swenson (former Linfield professor of economics) created their own company, FEI Corporation, in 1971. FEI initially set out "to provide high-purity, oriented single crystal materials for field emission research." By 2006 (a year in which it posted revenues of $479.5 million), it had diversified into nanotechnology and microscale biological research.

Following a similar sense of the possible instilled during their student experience at LRI, Linfield alumni Bill Mackie '71 (still a professor of physics) and Gary Cabe '72 founded Applied Physics Technologies (Aptech) in 1995. By 2006 the booming company had moved from Mackie's property into a 10,500-square-foot structure in McMinnville's industrial park. Both FEI and Aptech continue to provide unmatched opportunities for students to test themselves as active researchers.

scholarship. Computer use occurred mainly in the sciences and in a fledgling computer science major aligned with the mathematics department. Because Bull had once worked for Bell Laboratories and recognized that information technology would transform learning across all disciplines, she saw to it that the entire campus was wired to allow each department and office to exploit the Internet's vast potential. She also tackled other outmoded campus technologies. When Vice President for Finance Dale Tomlinson proudly informed her that the college had completed payment on its telephone switchboard, she decided to replace it with a computer-assisted system offering electronic voice mail and direct inward dialing. Since its founding three years before the first transcontinental telegraph line began operation in 1861, Linfield had seen steady and dramatic change in its communications with the outside world. Under Bull, that change accelerated as expanding electronic capabilities transformed operations within and beyond the classroom.

Just as Leonard Riley's success had enabled Elam Anderson to attend to the instructional program, Charles Walker's effectiveness led the trustees to charge Bull with strengthening academic quality, assuring her that she would face, at most, only one major building project. Like all history, Linfield's has its share of ironies—none perhaps greater than that by the end of her thirteen-year tenure, Bull would become a "building president" second only to Harry Dillin.

First, however, President Bull faced a number of initial challenges, some predictable and others not. She addressed growing campus advocacy of gay rights by meeting openly with the student group Fusion and posting a pink triangle inside her own office door to mark it as a welcoming space for gays in the Linfield community. In 1995, her administration's championing of equal rights for gays and lesbians, as endorsed by a vote of the faculty, resulted in an amendment to college policy prohibiting discrimination on the basis of sexual orientation. In keeping with a tradition of inclusive-

Left: *2004, Dr. Vivian A. Bull, president, 1992 to 2005, with students* ness and freedom of conscience, the several American Baptist clergy members of the Board of Trustees unanimously supported this Methodist president's new policy, though some lay members lamented that in their view the move contradicted Christian teachings.

While muted in comparison to the outcry against perceived radicalism that had greeted the early Bjork presidency, Bull's support for gay rights upset some in the local community who feared she might be steering the college away from its traditional values. These concerns deepened when the new president faced accusations, as had Bjork, that she sought to de-emphasize athletics. Some of this fear stemmed from increasingly selective admissions practices, one fruit of Linfield's enhanced academic reputation that won strong faculty support. As the number of students rejected by the college increased, however, some alumni contended that the situation hurt athletes disproportionately. Prospects of a move from the comfortable but disintegrating NAIA to the more robust NCAA Division III (which prohibited athletic scholarships) provoked consternation that the move would cripple Linfield's athletic prospects. Unfortunately, the debate hardened into a simplified either/or divide between academics and athletics that worsened such fears.

On its own, Linfield's continuance of its winning ways might have provided sufficient evidence that President Bull did not intend to de-emphasize athletics. But two distinct yet intertwined struggles erupted over Title IX that brought the leadership in athletics and the senior administration into direct conflict. Bull found herself named in a lawsuit filed by Professor Cindy Pemberton, swimming coach and an assistant director of athletics, who alleged personal discriminatory treatment and violation of Title IX in the college's plans for increasing women students' athletic opportunities. Concurrently, Bull became the target of an ad hoc group of sports-booster alumni who demanded her ouster under the rallying cry "POLE"–an acronym for "Protect Our Linfield Experience." On the other side of the gender equity debate from Pemberton, POLE asserted that enhancements to the

2007, Jereld R. Nicholson Library

Connecting Learning
The Library: Nook to Nicholson

In the early days of McMinnville College, President G.J. Burchett claimed library holdings would only "fill the apron of a generous old maid." In the original drafty building that housed the college, the library occupied a mere nook. After opening in 1883, Pioneer Hall housed the library for fifty-three years. The building gave respite from the wind and rain but offered little in the way of intellectual inspiration, for the collection totaled a scant 515 volumes.

Through the 1890s the collection reached 1,666 volumes—though many, having been contributed by clergy, dealt with theology, a subject not yet taught at the college. An accreditation table from 1922 lists volumes at "11,000 approx.," well below the 19,000 then deemed necessary for a college to rank other than "poor." Until 1937, faculty or staff with other college responsibilities assumed the additional duties associated with the library. Dr. William Frerichs supervised the library for ten years before the tasks of librarian and registrar fell to J. Kenneth Riley, the president's son.

During the 1930s Linfield benefited from the generosity of the Carnegie Corporation, and by the end of the decade library holdings increased to 29,000. At a golf outing in 1934, then Professor of Economics Harry L. Dillin suggested to President Elam Anderson that funding for a new library might be available from the federal Public Works Administration. Because private denominational colleges did not qualify, the college deeded the land to the city of McMinnville, which applied for and won the grant. The Emanuel Northup Library opened in 1936, with the city extending a ninety-nine-year lease to the college. In turn, Linfield expanded borrowing privileges so that "members of the community may use the library without paying any more fees than those charged the college students." After student fees became part of a uniform tuition in 1969, community members received free library privileges, a situation that continues to this day.

Northup Library became the responsibility of the college's first full-time librarian, Carolyn Smith (1937 to 1959). Its floor space expanded from 9,000 to 26,000 square feet in 1962, at which time the city also deeded the property back to the college. By 1998, however, the library's 118,000 books and 210,000 journal volumes had squeezed out all but 200 spaces for students to study. For decades a book had to be discarded for every new book acquired. The situation found long-awaited relief with the opening of the spacious and inviting Jereld R. Nicholson Library in fall 2003. The building is named for a 1939 Linfield history graduate who spent his life ranching in Dufur, Oregon. Nicholson left the college an estate valued at $6.4 million—to date, the largest gift from an individual.

Thanks to membership in the Orbis-Cascade Alliance, which combines resources from some thirty-four Oregon and Washington colleges and universities, Linfield students today enjoy access to 26.8 million volumes. They may also consult numerous electronic databases accessing scholarly journals. Through their leadership in this consortium, library directors Lynn Chmelir (1978 to 1999) and Susan Whyte (1999 to present) have provided an inestimable boost to the college's academic vitality.

Dr. Jane McIlroy   *Ad Rutschman*

Connecting Life
Coracing as Teaching

Coaching as Teaching

In 1913 President Leonard Riley appointed Professor Van Osdel of the science department as the college's first director of athletics. From that time until 1997, nearly all Linfield head coaches also belonged to the faculty. In 1997 the college began requiring PhDs of all new faculty appointments in the Department of Health and Human Performance. In reality, the increasing research and teaching expectations for new faculty also conflicted with the duties involved in effective coaching.

Among the several generations of productive faculty member/coaches at Linfield, two in particular merit special attention.

When Jane McIlroy arrived at Linfield in 1950 with a BA from Wheaton College and an MA from the University of Oregon, she entered a college where women's intercollegiate athletics consisted only of informal "Sports Days." Having spent three years in the Women's Army Corps helping to organize the military's first women's sports teams, she quickly set about developing organized intercollegiate athletic opportunities for Linfield's women students. Not only did she coach five varsity sports at Linfield, but she partnered with other institutions to form the Women's Conference of Independent Colleges. Twice she served as conference president.

Examples of McIlroy's commitment to excellence abound. While serving as women's athletic director from 1950 to 1982, she won conference championships as a coach in women's basketball, field hockey, tennis, track and field, and volleyball. She found time to earn her doctorate in education from Indiana University in 1961. On her retirement in 1982, her pioneering achievements merited a special award from the national convention of the Association for Intercollegiate Athletics for Women. To this day, the annual McIlroy-Lewis Award in the Northwest Athletic Conference recognizes the college with the top overall performance in both men's and women's competition.

As a student at Linfield, Ad Rutschman lettered for four years in football, basketball, and baseball and was named a Little All-American in football for the 1952 season. He coached at Hillsboro High School before succeeding his mentor, Paul Durham, as Linfield's head football coach in 1968. With Roy Helser's retirement as baseball coach in 1971, Rutschman assumed those head coaching duties as well, and won the national NAIA baseball title in his first year. Helser, who became athletic director after Durham, retired in 1973, leading to Rutschman's appointment to that position.

Amid such widespread accomplishments, football remains the sport where Rutschman left his most indelible coaching mark. Having won NAIA national championships in 1982, 1984, and 1986, he finished his football career in 1991 with a remarkable winning record of 183-48-3. He remains the only coach at any level to win national championships in two sports, and in 1998 he became the first-ever small college coach to be inducted into the National Football Hall of Fame in South Bend, Indiana.

In 1996, just before Ad's retirement, Linfield dedicated the Ad and Joan Rutschman Field House. The joint naming also recognized Rutschman's wife and longtime administrative assistant, Joan, for her contributions to his distinguished twenty-three years of service as athletic director.

women's athletic program would destroy competitiveness in men's programs, particularly football. President Bull confronted these challenges by drawing on deep reservoirs of personal calm and a strongly consultative leadership style. She patiently convened and reconvened all parties with a stake in the outcome, fostering honest dialogue so that, more often than not, a productive resolution might emerge.

These traits served her well as the inflamed passions on both sides peaked and eventually subsided. In the legal arena, Federal Magistrate Janice Stewart dismissed the Title IX portion of Pemberton's suit in a ruling on September 4, 1996, a decision upheld by U.S. District Judge Ancer Haggerty on December 2. The other discrimination charges were settled in a confidential agreement between Pemberton and college officers concluded in the following year. For its part, POLE pursued its own campaign of redress within existing institutional channels. Its members aggressively advocated that Ad Rutschman be persuaded to return as athletic director following his retirement at the end of 1996, but their letters to trustees achieved the opposite result when the board instead voted its confidence in President Bull by awarding her the first multiple-year contract ever given a Linfield president.

The POLE furor ebbed under the leadership of longtime baseball coach Scott Carnahan, who was tapped to become the new athletic director. Under Carnahan, numerous additional opportunities opened for intercollegiate women's athletics, including a new varsity women's lacrosse team—the first in the conference. In 2001, Linfield won its first-ever McIlroy-Lewis All Sports Trophy, awarded by the Northwest Athletic Conference to the school with the best overall record in both men's and women's sports. By repeating as winner of the trophy in 2003 and 2004, Linfield confirmed its continuing competitiveness in men's varsity sports and the growing competitiveness of its women's teams.

In the academic arena, Bull had hired Dr. Marvin Henberg of the University of Idaho to become dean of faculty and guide the development of a thoroughly revised general education curriculum. In 1997 the Faculty Assembly adopted a program of inquiry learning that recast familiar disciplinary distribution requirements in terms of cross-departmental "habits of mind." For instance, historical study in the area of inquiry known as "The Vital Past" predominantly featured courses in history, but also contained courses in literature and philosophy taught from a historical perspective. The new curricular categories also emphasized how different disciplines shared common questions about the human condition and the physical universe. The primary innovation of the new curriculum lay in the creation of the first-year Inquiry Seminar (IQS)—an academic apprenticeship for all incoming students. Taught by faculty members from across campus, the IQS develops students' critical skills in writing, speaking, and information gathering. Spurred by this same interdisciplinary commitment, Henberg also spearheaded creation of a new major in environmental studies, adopted in 2001.

In another initiative meant to build upon long-held Linfield practices, President Bull established a starting endowment of more than $1 million to support student-faculty collaborative research. Though already a staple of the science curriculum, contemporary faculty-led student research now required new levels of institutional funding. Bull recognized how such opportunities would keep the college competitive for top students and continue the impressive historical track record of Linfield science graduates pursuing doctoral study. Moreover, she sought to encourage faculty outside the sciences to develop their own approaches to collaborative research in their disciplines. Especially innovative was her funding of student participation at professional conferences in their fields—a vital means of fostering their interest in postbaccalaurate education.

Bull also understood that retaining the strong faculty being recruited to the college required expanded faculty development funds, and during her tenure she more than doubled such monies. Growing numbers of retirements, combined with new faculty positions added to serve a growing student body, produced dramatic change in faculty ranks.

2007, Linfield's NCAA Division III national softball champions hold high their trophy. Back row, left to right: *Jenny Marshall, Samantha Van Noy, Amanda Attleberger, Kendra Strahm, Jessica Bock, Jessica Popiel.* Front row, left to right: *Meredith Brunette, Brittany Miller, Jenessa Peterson, Stephanie Rice, Erica Hancock, Lisa Smith, Jena Loop, Candice Fujino, Danielle Stratton, Rochelle Friend, Rachelle Willden*

Scott Carnahan, athletic director, 1996 to present

As the scholarly activity expected of faculty members for promotion and tenure increased, the resources to support their efforts needed to increase as well. Bull secured board approval to create a faculty development endowment targeted for $1 million, three-quarters of which was raised before she left office in June 2005. Attainment of the full $1-million goal occurred in spring 2007 during Dr. Thomas Hellie's first year as Linfield's next president.

The hiring of so many new faculty during Bull's presidency produced a birthing blitz that echoed, in miniature, the post-World War II baby boom over which President Dillin had presided. This time, however, the parents of all the new infants stood in front of the classrooms, not in the seats. In

one year alone, Bull welcomed thirteen new babies to the Linfield brood.

What would most assuredly define the Bull legacy at Linfield, however, was the college's dramatic physical expansion —a result of fortuitous events occurring outside the college but ably managed through the teamwork of her cabinet and the board. Even Bull's early efforts in this regard exceeded the modest proportions outlined by the trustees at her hiring. Within her first three years at the college, she completed fund-raising or bonding for twice the number of new buildings projected in 1992: a new residence hall, South (now Mahaffey) Hall, opened in fall 2004, and the Rutschman Field House followed in spring 2005. Planning also proceeded for a long-awaited art, theatre, and music complex to be located across Cozine Creek on the former Columbus School property, which the college acquired in 1994. Behind the scenes, a new capital campaign to support the arts center and other needs took shape, but an outside consultant advised the administration that the Linfield Advancement Plan had tapped out potential resources for the time being. Bull was thus advised to pursue a comprehensive fund-raising target of $28 million, $6 million less than the goal of Walker's last campaign.

While into the silent phase of this new effort, however, Bull received surprising news: in October 1996 the Hewlett-Packard Corporation informed her privately that it planned to close its McMinnville manufacturing facility, located on 105 acres contiguous to the south boundary of campus. Originally acquired by Walter Dyke, first for the Linfield Research Institute and then for Femcor, the property's future appeared up for grabs, raising the prospect it could be "brought home" to Linfield College itself. Initially, however, HP made clear

Opposite: The Spanish classroom mural in Walker Hall, painted in 1993 by Professor of Art Ron Mills, with ceramics by Professor of Art Nils Lou. The mural depicts iconographic moments in Mesoamerican myth and history. A leader in expanding Linfield's international outreach, Mills has painted equally striking murals at sister universities in Costa Rica and Mexico.

Connecting Life
Waiting and "Waiting"

As an inherently collaborative undertaking, theatre embodies and enacts Linfield's commitment to learning, life, and community. With origins in myth and religious ceremony, theatre holds up a mirror that reveals human complexity and contradiction. As a result, it regularly challenges the proprieties safeguarded by public authorities of all stripes.

Theatre at Linfield sprang from the college's late-nineteenth-century Philergian, Nicaian, and Philomethean societies, where rhetorical contests led naturally to the staging of character-driven dramatic interactions. Even so, college authorities equivocated. They tolerated but did not endorse organization of a drama club in 1917. Forensics instruction lapsed during World War I, with faculty members generally recruited by students to coach and direct. Professor George Varney assumed responsibility for theatre on his return from the war, yielding in 1923 to the ebullient May Chalfant, professor of romance languages.

Perhaps because many conservative Baptists thought it of dubious moral standing, drama remained essentially itinerant for several decades. Productions were staged variously in town (the Lark Theatre or Old Opera House), in Music Hall, or occasionally in the Pioneer chapel. In 1928 the Melrose chapel (now Ice Auditorium) became something of a permanent home for theatre, but scheduling for the space competed with required chapel, music performance, public lectures, and forensic competitions.

Following World War II, the college secured the theatre at the Portland Air Base and moved it to campus to become the Fine Arts Building, later christened Frerichs Hall. The hall's Little Theatre proved a huge boon to the program, and productions of such standards as *Gaslight*, *Harvey*, *Arsenic and Old Lace*, and *My Three Angels* generated much interest. Playbills reflect faculty participation from across the college. A dedicated space also gave Professor Roy Mahaffey room to work with his Vesper Players, who staged liturgical drama throughout the region.

2003, Professor Tyrone Marshall and President Vivian Bull lead a processional away from the theatre department's "temporary quarters" in Pioneer Hall.

Theatre's itinerant origins returned, not as farce but as tragedy, when Frerichs Hall burned to the ground on December 16, 1969. Pioneer Hall's two-story interior space (once the chapel), offered as a "temporary" solution, would house the theatre program for the next thirty-four years. The faculty and students made the best of a very difficult situation, since the space allowed only portable shop equipment and a scant sixty-five-seat house set on risers. Yet in these same years six Linfield students received invitations to compete in the prestigious American Festival Theatre Competition at the Kennedy Center in Washington, D.C. Two won top national honors in their categories.

The first and last play produced in the Pioneer Theatre, *Waiting for Godot*, dramatizes the tension between hope and despair that playwright Samuel Beckett believed defined the modern human condition. In May 2003, after striking the set in Pioneer Hall, joyous students and faculty members paraded the copper tree created for the production by Professor Tyrone Marshall (himself a holder of a Kennedy Center Medallion) to its new home outside Ford Hall—the theatre the community had been waiting for since 1969.

that it would sell its McMinnville property to the highest bidder rather than give the college special consideration. Nonetheless, a tireless negotiating team of college officers and trustees, led by Bull, Vice President for Finance Carl Vance, Trustee David Jubb, and Trustee Secretary David Haugeberg, convinced HP's leadership of the transformative impact of this property for the college. The company agreed to sell seventeen acres plus the buildings that stood on them for $4.95 million. In addition HP donated seventy undeveloped acres, appraised at $5.6 million. The remainder of the full 105-acre HP tract came to Linfield in 2000 via a similar gift-purchase arrangement. All told, Hewlett-Packard's contributions to Linfield totaled $7.8 million, still the largest gift in the college's history.

This acquisition more than doubled the size of the campus, which went from 87 to 192 acres in two years. The goal of the capital campaign, now named The Defining Moment, grew to $65 million, including the resources needed to capitalize on the HP opportunities. Foundations, corporations, and private donors who had been out of reach earlier now responded to the exciting vision for Linfield made possible with such expanded physical resources. Through it all, President Bull kept enhanced institutional excellence as her rallying cry for the new campaign. Over its seven-and-one-half-year run, The Defining Moment raised just under $74 million, an unprecedented result for an institution of historically modest means.

A building spree on the scale of Linfield's post-World War II era thus began to reshape Linfield College. Campus infrastructure saw the most immediate improvements. The old power plant, a relic of Dillin's early presidency, was replaced by a new central steam plant whose pipelines snaked out across the enlarged campus. Six new apartment-style residence halls boasting private bedrooms, washers, dryers, and full Internet access appeared in the appropriately named Hewlett Packard Park. The new Withnell Commons housed a relocated post office and meeting spaces for students. Facility Services relocated to a remodeled former

Hewlett-Packard Corporation physical plant building.

Instructional and academic spaces saw dramatic additions as well. Dean Henberg suggested developing an arts quadrangle on part of the HP property by combining new construction with renovation of existing buildings. The James F. Miller Fine Arts Center opened in two of those remodeled structures (including LRI's original Linke Hall) in 2001. The long-awaited state-of-the-art Nicholson Library opened alongside Ford Hall (home of the Marshall Theatre) in an adjacent building renovation in 2003. In 2006, President Emerita Bull presided at the dedication of the Vivian A. Bull Music Center. This new structure, like Marshall Theatre, finally restored professional-caliber teaching facilities to a department that had lost them to fire three decades earlier. The seventeen acres immediately surrounding the arts quadrangle have been collectively named the Keck Campus, in honor of a key contribution from the W.M. Keck Foundation of Los Angeles that had made these improvements possible.

Above: *2007, Laura Sibley at a potter's wheel in the James F. Miller Fine Arts Center*

Opposite: *2007, The Hewlett Packard apartments on a spring day*

Many contributions to The Defining Moment campaign were sacrificial for the givers—as, for instance, board chairman Richard Ice's donation of $1 million for the Richard and Lucille Ice Auditorium in Melrose Hall. Adding one dollar to the Ice pledge, trustee Richard Withnell gave another million to honor his father, Harold Withnell, class of 1939. Neither Ice nor Withnell possessed the personal wealth generally associated with seven-figure gifts. Whether measured by continuing reliance on student labor, the unstinting commitment from faculty and staff, or financial gifts of real personal sacrifice, the saga of Linfield College rides high on contributions of talent, time, and treasure from those who love her.

A closer look at one such contribution provides an apt conclusion, not only to Bull's presidency but also to the historical narrative of Linfield's first hundred and fifty years. It is the story of Jereld R. Nicholson, whose name is memorialized in the new library. Graduating from Linfield in 1939 with a degree in history, Nicholson left his Depression-era alma mater for employment at the Underhill Ranch in Dufur, Oregon, first as a ranch hand and later as foreman. He eventually became its owner, and outsiders presumed the ranch to be his primary, if not his sole, asset. Quietly, however, in good years and in bad, Nicholson bought stocks from the proceeds of his cattle sales. He selected stocks wisely and held on to them, trusting his initial judgment. Meanwhile he supported Linfield with small gifts and by recommending it to students from central and eastern Oregon. Only on his death in 2002 did the college learn that his now sizable estate had been transmitted to the college. Nicholson's generosity created the largest gift the college has yet received from an individual: $6.4 million.

Summing up President Bull's many accomplishments invites a return to earlier history. Like Elam Anderson before her, she followed a president who effectively saved the college. As with Anderson, an influential college constituency once again strenuously challenged her leadership. While Anderson had taken his talents elsewhere in the face of such opposition, however, President Bull endured and prevailed. In consequence, she created a rich legacy of her own: enhanced support for faculty scholarship and creative activity, reliable support for undergraduate student/faculty collaborative research, a campus doubled in size, and robust new facilities, especially for the arts and the library.

Quiet, unafraid of hard work, pragmatically persistent, inspired by the liberating potential of education—all these traits characterized Jereld R. Nicholson. Given how deeply rooted those values remain in the ethos of the institution, it seems likely that they will characterize Linfield graduates for the next hundred and fifty years and beyond. ■

Connecting Learning
Buildings Named for Faculty

When each generation arrives in McMinnville, students learn building names primarily for ease in navigating. Yet students threading their way through campus also move through layers of history. Among the more than forty buildings named for significant contributors to the college, eleven honor faculty members, nine celebrate trustees, eight cite pioneers or local community members (see "Community Place Names on Campus," p. 33), five acknowledge presidents, and five thank benefactors.

Fittingly, the largest such category honors those who served the college primarily as teachers. The first faculty member to merit a named building, Isabel Grover (p. 36), has been joined by ten additional faculty members. Vignettes on Carrie Potter (p. 48), Emanuel Northup (p. 37), William R. Frerichs (p. 86), and Ad Rutschman (p. 126) appear elsewhere in this volume. The remaining faculty members earn mention below.

Herschel Hewitt, professor of physics, had a residence hall dedicated in his name in 1960. A graduate of Grand Island College with an MS from the University of Chicago, Hewitt taught from 1921 to 1946. His early years of practical experience as an assayer for mining companies in northern Idaho led him to teach in the practical, hands-on manner that endeared him to many generations of Linfield students, among them Walter Dyke and Kenneth Trolan, founders of the Linfield Research Institute.

Luther R. Taylor, professor of chemistry, drew recognition when a building moved from the Portland Air Base in 1947 received his name in 1961. A 1915 McMinnville College graduate, Taylor received his MS from Washington State College before returning to teach at his alma mater from 1928 until 1958. Known for demanding the best from his students, he earned their affection for his "warm friendship and personal help."

E. Avard Whitman, member of the English faculty and longtime registrar, was honored by a new residence hall dedicated in 1966. With a BA from Linfield (1921), he went on to earn his MA and PhD from the University of Washington. He joined the English faculty in 1938 and became registrar in 1941, splitting his time between those duties and teaching English until his death in 1964. As registrar for twenty-three years, he encountered virtually every student of the college.

Roy D. "Hap" Mahaffey, professor of speech and drama, ties with Harold Elkinton for longevity among faculty members honored by a building name. Another alumnus, he served his alma mater for 42 years from his graduation in 1928 until 1970. He earned his MA at the University of Southern California. Inheriting a strong forensics tradition, he made it even stronger. A specialist in religious drama and founder of the local Vesper Players, Mahaffey directed and acted in hundreds of plays of all types. He received an honorary doctorate from Linfield in 1960. The former South Hall, built in 1994, became Mahaffey Hall in 2003.

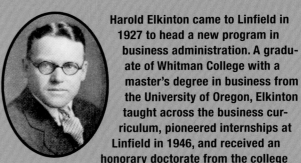

Harold Elkinton came to Linfield in 1927 to head a new program in business administration. A graduate of Whitman College with a master's degree in business from the University of Oregon, Elkinton taught across the business curriculum, pioneered internships at Linfield in 1946, and received an honorary doctorate from the college in 1960. Known to generations of students as "Elkie" or "The Elk," he retired in 1969. Elkinton Hall joined the college's dormitory roster in 2006.

Horace C. "Hod" Terrell, a graduate of Earlham College, came to Linfield in 1933 after earning his MA in English from the University of Oregon. He received his PhD from the University of Washington in 1938. A devout Quaker, he took leave during World War II to volunteer for the American Red Cross. His influence operated primarily in the classroom, as indicated by the decision to dedicate the 1955 *Oak Leaves* in honor of his teaching excellence. He retired in 1961. Terrell Hall, another dormitory, opened in 2006.

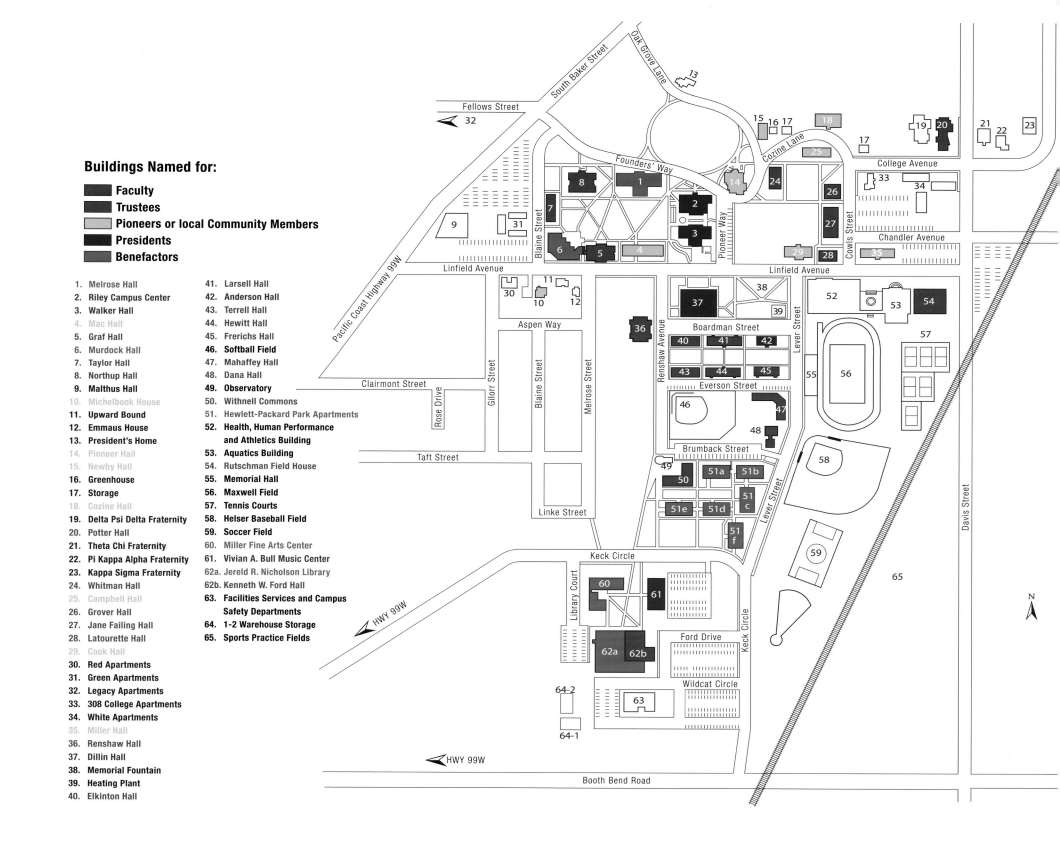

Buildings Named for:

Faculty
Trustees
Pioneers or local Community Members
Presidents
Benefactors

1. Melrose Hall
2. Riley Campus Center
3. Walker Hall
4. Mac Hall
5. Graf Hall
6. Murdock Hall
7. Taylor Hall
8. Northup Hall
9. Malthus Hall
10. Michelbook House
11. Upward Bound
12. Emmaus House
13. President's Home
14. Pioneer Hall
15. Newby Hall
16. Greenhouse
17. Storage
18. Cozine Hall
19. Delta Psi Delta Fraternity
20. Potter Hall
21. Theta Chi Fraternity
22. Pi Kappa Alpha Fraternity
23. Kappa Sigma Fraternity
24. Whitman Hall
25. Campbell Hall
26. Grover Hall
27. Jane Failing Hall
28. Latourette Hall
29. Cook Hall
30. Red Apartments
31. Green Apartments
32. Legacy Apartments
33. 308 College Apartments
34. White Apartments
35. Miller Hall
36. Renshaw Hall
37. Dillin Hall
38. Memorial Fountain
39. Heating Plant
40. Elkinton Hall

41. Larsell Hall
42. Anderson Hall
43. Terrell Hall
44. Hewitt Hall
45. Frerichs Hall
46. Softball Field
47. Mahaffey Hall
48. Dana Hall
49. Observatory
50. Withnell Commons
51. Hewlett-Packard Park Apartments
52. Health, Human Performance and Athletics Building
53. Aquatics Building
54. Rutschman Field House
55. Memorial Hall
56. Maxwell Field
57. Tennis Courts
58. Helser Baseball Field
59. Soccer Field
60. Miller Fine Arts Center
61. Vivian A. Bull Music Center
62a. Jereld R. Nicholson Library
62b. Kenneth W. Ford Hall
63. Facilities Services and Campus Safety Departments
64. 1-2 Warehouse Storage
65. Sports Practice Fields

Dr. Stephen Bricher turns mathematics into an adventure. As he paces through the classroom, firing questions with a smile that compels attention, every particle of his lean, six-foot-six-inch frame exudes joy at quantifying the world.

Bricher holds a PhD in mathematics from the University of Colorado. A 1986 summa cum laude Linfield graduate, Bricher follows in a proud line of fine math and science educators who have returned to teach at their alma mater. He has twice won the Edith Green Distinguished Professor Award and has pioneered the contemporary expansion in collaborative student-faculty research at Linfield. His passion lies in employing partial differential equations to model complex phenomena such as gaseous explosions. To his students, explosions in knowledge have become routine.

Dr. Jill Timmons wraps teaching, performance, and scholarship into a single vibrant whole. With her BA and BM from the University of Washington, MM from Boston University, and DMA from the University of Washington, Timmons has distinguished herself as scholar as well as musician. With Sylvain Fremaux she coauthored *Alexandre Tansman: Diary of a Twentieth Century Composer*, winner of the Wilk Prize from the University of Southern California.

Followers of Ken Burns's 2007 PBS documentary on World War II will have sampled her talent, for among her four CD piano recordings, one—*The Music of Amy Beach* (performed with Laura Klugherz)—comprises a portion of that production's sound track. In addition to recruiting and teaching numerous outstanding Linfield piano students, Timmons has taught master classes in many universities and academies throughout the United States and Europe.

Dave Hansen's passions range from teaching economics to cultivating new generations of leaders. In the latter capacity he has served since 1988 as Linfield's dean of students. Many know him best as the radio "voice of the [football and basketball] Wildcats." He recalls missing only three football games since becoming a broadcaster.

Holding a BS from Willamette University and an MS from Portland State University, Professor Hansen joined the Linfield community in 1969. When asked about inspirational Linfield educators, alumni name him more often than anyone else at the college. Sometimes the admiration of students stems directly from his having provoked them to serious self-assessment by giving them poor grades in his classes or inviting them to an interview in his office. Hansen has offered seminars on leadership for the Ford Family Foundation and to various Oregon chambers of commerce and public agencies. His career typifies the blending of theory and practice that Linfield espouses, as he has held the presidency of the McMinnville Chamber of Commerce and has served as a McMinnville city councillor, with 2007 marking his seventh year in office.

Dr. Howard Leichter exemplifies the rising scholarly profile of Linfield faculty in recent decades. A renowned authority on the comparative politics of health care, Leichter regularly receives invitations to speak at academic and governmental conferences in Asia, America, and Europe. His book, *Free to Be Foolish: The Politics of Health Promotion,* published in 1991 by Princeton University Press, remains a standard reference in its field. His accomplishments will in fact provide benchmarks for scholarly endeavor among his peers far into the future.

Holding a BA from City University of New York, an MA from the University of Hawaii, and a PhD from the University of Wisconsin, Leichter has excelled as teacher as well as researcher. He earned the Edith Green Distinguished Professor Award and has counseled many of the college's Fulbright Scholarship winners, not to mention generations of future attorneys and academicians. His students know well his intolerance for shoddy work and also know that those who strive to put out their best effort—and extend what they thought themselves capable of—will find the light in his Pioneer office ablaze and welcoming.

Dr. Barbara May mobilizes her students to constructive intervention whenever they confront women patients who have been physically or emotionally abused. As a teacher she finds it insufficient simply to treat the symptoms of suffering. An uncompromising activist, she doggedly pursues resources to illuminate and redress the underlying social conditions of abuse that exist beyond the clinic doors. Her volunteer spirit, fired by hope and moral obligation, offers a powerful antidote to the apathy, fatalism, or fear that can frequently limit societal responses to the problems faced by battered women.

With a BSN from Trenton State College, an MN from Montana State University, and a PhD from Oregon Health & Science University, Barbara May earned the Samuel H. Graf Faculty Achievement Award in 1994. As an accomplished researcher within the nursing faculty, she generously invited many of her colleagues into partnership, producing a series of coauthored, referred publications and ultimately inspiring her colleagues to pursue their own research. She currently coleads a major initiative to attract nursing students from a greater diversity of ethnic and socioeconomic backgrounds.

Chipo Dendere, 2007-08 president of the Associated Students of Linfield College, merits recognition in part for being the first international student to occupy that post. A native of Harare, Zimbabwe, Dendere has chosen majors in both political science and psychology, and she has already distinguished herself with faculty in both areas as a valued collaborative researcher. She is also an accomplished member of the college's forensics team and a valued contributor to the work of the International Programs Office. Her leadership position with ASLC represents an already stellar track record that has made her a welcome presence in a wide variety of campus venues.

Such accomplishments in pursuit of a U.S. education prove all the more commendable in the face of geopolitical efforts to levy sanctions against Zimbabwe's repressive government. No wonder that Dendere's electoral platform emphasized unity—a unity of global understanding and a unity on campus among groups with diverse beliefs and commitments. A prestigious 2007 summer internship at the Carter Center in Atlanta, Georgia, made possible by the Allen and Pat Kelley Achievement Award, provided another opportunity for her to hone her already considerable leadership skills.

Afterword
Inspired Pragmatism in Linfield's Future

By Barbara Kitt Seidman

At Linfield we will continue to connect learning, life, and community. We will do it by focusing on the liberal arts, by integrating them with professional programs, by linking theory with experience, by serving and studying our local community, by embracing multicultural diversity, by studying abroad, and by striving for excellence in all our endeavors. These ideas are not new to Linfield—you were committed to these values long before I arrived—but I can promise that I will do my best to embrace, defend, and champion them.

From the Inaugural Address of President Thomas L. Hellie

On March 2, 2007, Board of Trustees chairperson Glenna Kruger formally invested Dr. Thomas L. Hellie with the presidency of Linfield College. The search for a worthy successor to President Vivian Bull had taken nearly two years, and into the breach between Bull's departure and Hellie's arrival stepped Dean of Faculty Dr. Marv Henberg, who, at the invitation of the trustees, served as acting president from July 1, 2005, through April 1, 2006. Hellie began his tenure on April 2. Eager to learn about the college from the ground up, he quickly confirmed for himself the wisdom of his decision to leave Chicago's Kemper Foundation to become Linfield's nineteenth president.

After months of one-on-one conversations with the faculty, job-sharing with employees from other sectors of the college, and encounters with students over meals in Dillin Hall, Hellie told the assembled audience at the fall 2006 opening convocation that Linfield had many reasons to be proud of its strong regional reputation—and that it could not rest on those laurels but must strive to keep renewing and reinventing itself in the face of new challenges. In his inaugural address some six months later, he cautioned that

2007, President Thomas L. Hellie delivers his inaugural address.

"excellence is always a goal, never completely achieved. . . . One cannot be complacent or relax. You always have to work harder, or you're going to fall behind." This passion to move Linfield forward unites President Hellie with the community he now leads.

Inspired by predecessors who saw the college's untapped potential as the key to its uncharted future, today's citizens of Linfield College continue its legacy of inspired pragmatism. As proof, in fall 2006 the faculty ratified three Foundational Education Principles that emphasize integrative thinking, global and multicultural perspectives, and experiential learning as central to responsible undergraduate preparation for the twenty-first century. None of these principles will strike readers as unfamiliar, but all three call for further innovation if Linfield is to reach generations of new students who expect to learn by doing. In that way more than any other, Linfield will extend its influence in the wider world.

No one person articulates the full vision of what Linfield might become: as always, the necessary ideas and energy originate from every part of a community whose employees proudly and on a daily basis serve its institutional mission. In the coming decade alone, Linfield will undertake an impressive array of projects to foster that mission. Northup Hall, once the library and a nexus of town-gown intellectual exchange, will undergo extensive renovation to become a vibrant integrated educational center housing the departments of business, economics, English, and philosophy. Planning has also begun for a long-needed redesign and expansion of existing science facilities—a major undertaking for any institution, but one absolutely vital to the continuing success of science education at Linfield, given the school's strong history of placing graduates in medical and research careers. A newly launched Linfield Center for Regional Studies promises cross-disciplinary engagement among faculty members and with community leaders from an array of backgrounds, with its ultimate goal the expansion of experiential learning opportunities for students. The Portland Campus also stands poised for transformation to respond to looming shortages among health care professionals in the coming years.

The classroom itself has evolved into a very different place from that experienced by most Linfield alumni, and such changes will only accelerate. A technology-phobic literature teacher like myself who still prefers paperback books to a laptop has trouble fathoming, let alone describing, the digital wizardry that can bring the entire known past as well as the vast contemporary world into real-time interaction with students. Not that all of Linfield's classrooms are bounded by walls: online course delivery has redefined distance

Historic Northup Hall awaits remodeling.

learning, as evidenced by the international enrollments now occurring in the Division of Continuing Education. Given the possibilities unleashed by these new pedagogies, many faculty are already experimenting with e-portfolios to allow students to archive and assess evidence of their own intellectual growth over time—even as faculty review those same portfolios for valuable insights into the fit between curriculum and actual learning.

The international breadth that has long defined "The Linfield Experience" continues to expand as new semester-abroad sites become available and January Term course offerings diversify to as many compass points as creative faculty can devise. One impressive statistic offers a glimpse at the impact of such experiences upon our students: in the short span of a decade (1997 to 2007), fifteen Linfield graduates have earned prestigious national Fulbright awards sending them to study in Eastern and Western Europe, South and Central America, Northern and sub-Saharan Africa, and Australia. Such a result, recently commended in the *Chronicle of Higher Education,* required more than just superb student candidates (although of course they are the essential ingredient): overall, dozens of faculty mentors devoted time and energy to encouraging the applicants. And at the helm stood Professor Deborah Olsen, competitive scholarships advisor, who shepherded each application through the many hoops of a complicated process.

Nowhere do Linfield's winning ways emerge more clearly than in its proud athletics tradition, but that too needs regular refreshing and reinvention to achieve new heights—continuing The Streak alone will not suffice. Former Yankee Scott Brosius, a Linfield graduate in 2002 and most valuable player in the 1998 World Series, has taken over the head coaching position in baseball, for example, and the 2007 national champion softball Wildcats look forward to defending their title far into the future. Meanwhile the college is planning construction of a new facility to support its teams' conditioning needs as well as the pedagogical demands of its distinctive athletic training major—a program where

2007, Director of International Programs Shaik Ismail, President Thomas L. Hellie, Dean of Faculty Barbara Seidman, and Professor of Philosophy Marvin Henberg command the front row in a reenactment of the 1890s community photographs from The Baptist College at McMinnville (see p. 36).

commensurate with its aspirations. Here too, the gains of recent decades will not suffice to keep Linfield competitive in an age where modestly endowed colleges stand in perpetual jeopardy of falling behind in delivering quality education of the kind Linfield has exemplified throughout its history.

Sometimes the consequences of a constricted endowment operate beneath the surface of what the public sees. Successful private liberal arts education rests on a crucial conjunction of engaged faculty and industrious students, all of whom must find it within their means to remain part of the equation. Public institutions regularly promise faculty greater remuneration and wider opportunities for scholarly endeavor; they also offer lower price tags to potential enrollees. Wealthier private schools also compete for the most promising faculty and the most ambitious students. As senior faculty retire, Linfield's present salaries will doubtless prove insufficient to attract worthy successors. Nor does the college wish to lessen its cherished commitment to provide access to private education for students of modest means. Yet to ensure such access will require endowed scholarship funds far in excess of what currently exist. For all of these reasons, President Hellie has made endowment growth the foundation stone for building the future Linfield he described in his inaugural address.

Speaking as one who has belonged to this community of teachers and learners for almost a quarter century, I can say without equivocation that I have never felt more hopeful about its prospects. Linfield stands on the threshold of a new era, but one consistent with its finest impulses over a hundred-and-fifty-year history. Its distinctive blend of realism and creativity (or is it creative realism?) has kept it supple when less flexible institutions have broken, and yet its adherents have never ceased imagining how to improve on the educational experience offered its students. We who work here know it is always the students who compel our dedication and provide our most satisfying rewards. May future students reap the same rich rewards enjoyed by their precursors—riches documented so poignantly in these pages. The best is yet to come, and won't it be fine? ■

academic rigor, experiential learning, preprofessional training, and sport converge in distinctive Linfield fashion.

As this volume makes abundantly clear, the challenges of keeping Linfield's doors open have dogged the college since its inception. The limitations of an insufficient—indeed, at times nonexistent—endowment frequently crippled the college's ability to absorb periodic budget stresses or launch much-needed initiatives to deliver on its potential. Not surprisingly, then, President Hellie has made clear that in addition to the kinds of projects already described, he intends to commit himself to building an endowment for the college

Index of People, Places, and Organizations

Note to readers: Page numbers with *box* indicate vignettes. Page numbers in **bold type** indicate illustrations, their captions, or subjects of vignettes.